AMBITIOUS

One Man's Journey to Conquer the Darkness of Dyslexia

LIKEWISE
&
VELVET SKIES

INDIGORIVER
PUBLISHING

AMBITIOUS

Ambitious

Editors: Earl Tillinghast, Hamishe Randall , Regina Cornell

Cover Design: John Lucas

Interior Design: Whitney Evans, SGR-P Formatting

Indigo River Publishing 3 West Garden Street Ste. 352 Pensacola, FL 32502 www.indigoriverpublishing.com

Ordering Information:

Quantity sales: Special discounts are available on quantity purchases by corporations, associations, and others. For details, contact the publisher at the address above.

Orders by U.S. trade bookstores and wholesalers: Please contact the publisher at the address above.

Printed in the United States of America

Library of Congress Control Number: 2018934578

ISBN: 978-1-948080-14-9

First Edition

*With Indigo River Publishing, you can always expect great books, strong voices, and meaningful messages. Most importantly, you'll always find...*words worth reading.

Contents

Chapter One

M y name is Likewise. Everyone has a journey and
a story to tell. Welcome to mine...

I was born on a cold winter morning, January 8, 1967,
and grew up as the seventh child in what would become a
family of sixteen brothers and sisters, including me, and it
wasn't easy. We lived in the remote country farm town of
Stella, North Carolina, where there was only a gas station-
convenience store and a post office. It would take my
parents at least forty minutes to drive into the town of
Jacksonville, where the closest grocery stores, hospitals,
doctor's offices, and pharmacies were located.

The family started out in a three-bedroom, one-
bathroom trailer, and by the time I arrived, my father had
built on an extra bedroom for our growing family.

Both of my parents came from larger-than-average

families. My father was one of five children, and my mother was next to the last of seventeen. As the baby girl, not only did my mother's parents focus a great deal of attention on her, but her older siblings did as well, resulting in all of Mom's needs being met. By the time she entered the world, fewer kids were living at home; therefore, her experiences growing up may have been different from those of her older siblings, as I'm sure mine are from my youngest brothers and sisters.

As far as I know, my mother's family had money to pay bills and buy groceries and believed if they didn't earn it or grow it, they didn't need it. Older siblings helped younger ones, everyone had chores, and, of course, there was always someone to talk to or play with. I believe Mom focused on those positives of her youth and wanted the same for her own budding family. Without a doubt, she and my father taught my brothers, sisters, and me responsibility at an early age and emphasized we should look out for each other. However, financially my mother was in for a rude awakening. Even though she and my father sacrificed for our family, we often had little to eat and it was hard to stay warm at times. But my parents truly loved each other and us and did the best they could.

Prior to marrying, my mother had graduated from high school. And although my father had little formal education, I thought he was a genius because he had more worldly knowledge than a lot of college graduates. Both of my parents were sharp, and if there were ever such a place as *Harvard Worldly University*, Mom and Dad would have made straight As. In fact, my parents could have taught the curriculum.

Dad was part American Indian. He taught our family many useful survival skills, including how to catch rabbits and squirrels without using a gun, and there were times we needed his knowledge. One icy winter, we were snowed in for about two weeks and ran out of food. Snowdrifts were unusually high, making it dangerous for us children to go out, so Dad climbed under the trailer to retrieve several of the many traps we'd seen him build using scrap wood and string. They were approximately two feet long by seven inches wide. Because they were narrow and long, rabbits and squirrels couldn't turn around inside, and Dad could easily pull out his catch without being bitten. He would place the box-shaped devices about ten feet from the house. Each one had a string on the door and a stick on top of the trap with a bottle cap nailed to it to help guide the line. The string ran all the way to the windows of our home. Dad would then leave a trail of moldy bread on top of the snow leading into the trap. When my siblings and I saw a rabbit or squirrel follow the path of bait inside, we'd yank the string and capture the animal. Jumping up and down, like clowns in a circus, we would yell with delight; we were so happy to catch dinner! Unfortunately,

LIKEWISE & VELVET SKIES

some days we didn't eat at all, but we watched out for each other.

Because we lived far away from modern conveniences and money was tight, my father would often venture into the close-by woods, gather ingredients such as wild onions, tree bark, and wild cherries, boil them and make medicines for us. If a bee stung us, he would take tobacco, chew it up, and place it on the bee sting to draw the stinger out, and then the swelling would go down. When one of my brothers cut his hand, Dad used tree sap to seal the wound.

My father was a master at innovation. He would often sharpen knives by repeatedly stabbing them in the ground or replace a broken pipe using a radiator hose. Once, he made a plow out of four 10-speed bicycle rims by placing two on each side of a stick with cinder blocks in the center to help weigh it down so it would go into the dirt. It was a lot of work to push it, but was a much faster process than using a hoe to create rows in our big family garden. As kids, Dad taught us to make toy bows and arrows using tree branches and wire. And when we were older, I remember him designing flowerpots out of old tires: he would make cuts along a tire's inside edge, turn that side over, stand in the center, and flip the whole tire wrong side out. It was one of the coolest things I had ever seen. Neighbors would ask my mother about them. Therefore, Dad started making and selling them. My mother loved my father so much; to her, everything he created was gold.

Word spread of our large family, and when my father journeyed into Jacksonville, people would frequently give him bags of hand-me-downs. Originally, neither of my parents wanted them. My father would gratefully accept the donations, but he'd pass them to another needy family before heading home. However, as our family grew, so did our needs, and Dad began to tote home large black trash bags full of second-hand items. My mother had a lot of dignity and was initially so upset she would whirl the sacks out the front door, into the yard. Listening to her stories over the years, I understood why her family had never accepted handouts. She believed if her parents could raise a large family without help, then she and my father could too. But as money became tighter and tighter, Mom eventually swallowed some of her pride and allowed my brothers, sisters, and me to go through the used items. She noticed the smiles beam across our faces as we searched through clothes, shoes, and toys, as if we were pirates discovering treasure. As our family multiplied, Mom became increasingly happy to receive the items as well.

My mother was a great seamstress, and she could fashion the secondhand clothes to fit to a tee. I recall her making a tape measure to use for alterations by placing a yardstick on a wrong-side-out pair of jeans, marking the length, copying the measurements with an ink pen, then cutting the strip out. She'd spend hours measuring, cutting, and sewing the used garments by hand to make sure they fit us. She believed even though we were poor, we didn't have to look like it. She taught us to value ourselves and emphasized we shouldn't run around telling people what we didn't have, because that would only call attention to it.

With so many kids in an expanding family, it seemed my mother was always doing laundry. In our hallway was an old wringer washer, and she could regularly be found there, washing load after load. When the machine had run a cycle, she would remove the freshly cleaned clothes and feed one garment at a time through the wringer on top to remove excess water. Whenever the washer was on the blink and Dad couldn't afford a part, Mom had to resort to an even more old-fashioned way of washing.

She would head out back to fill a big tin washtub, large enough for an adult to sit in, half full of water from our hose, then gather our clothes and put like colors into the washtub to soak. She routinely flipped a five-gallon bucket upside down and placed it near to be used as a stool. Taking a seat on the bucket, she would insert a wooden-framed tin washboard into the tub. She proceed by picking up a piece of clothing and rubbing a bar of brown Lava soap all over it until a sudsy lather formed; then she'd scrub the piece vigorously back and forth over the ridges of the washboard until the item was clean. Mom wore out more than one washboard, and there were times when I

was honestly worried about her hands; I was afraid she
would eventually rub them off like an eraser on paper.

To rinse, Mom transferred the garments to a second
washtub half filled with water, agitated them with her
palms and fingers, and then lifted one item at a time to
allow excess liquid to drain before she tightly wrung each
out by hand. Next, she placed clean shirts, jeans, dresses,
etc., into a spick-and-span five-gallon lard bucket and
carried them to the clotheslines in our back yard, where
she normally hung them. At times, my older sisters
chipped in to help, as we all did with chores around
the house.

When I was quite young, I'd try to help my mother
carry the large bucket of wet clothes to the clotheslines,
but it was so heavy and I was so small I'd have to twist
and twirl it, placing hand over hand around the lip of the
bucket, just to attempt to get it across the yard. Many a
time, one of my big brothers would see my dilemma, grab
the bucket handle, and tote it the rest of the way.

Around the house, Mom would routinely play old jazz
and gospel records while tidying things up. Most of them
were given to her, warped and scratched. She would place
the warped ones near the stove until the heat caused them
to flatten, and she used rubbing alcohol on the scratches to
repair them as best she could. In spite of her efforts, the
record player needle would frequently get stuck, causing
the music to sound like Alvin and the Chipmunks, but

7

Mom didn't mind; she'd lift the needle, place it back down, and tunes continued to play. Mom enjoyed belting out the lyrics right on time with the music, and I recall thinking, *She really has a beautiful voice!*

One afternoon, while watching my mother go about her daily chores, my mind focused on her hard work and the sacrifices she regularly made. I realized Superman had nothing on her; not even kryptonite could slow my mom down! I smiled as I thought, *She must really love us.*

During summer breaks from school, my younger siblings and I were free to play after we completed jobs around the house. My older siblings who worked outside the home, sometimes cutting grass, other times farming, were expected to give Mom most of their earnings to go toward bills and groceries. At the end of the season, Mom and Dad would go into town with any remaining funds, and shop sales to pick out a few school clothes for my brothers, sisters, and me. My parents made all purchases; there were far too many of us to fit into a vehicle for a shopping trip.

Now and again, Mom would visit her mother and Dad would be at work, so my brothers, sisters, and I would run and skip down tree-covered nature trails to gather wild cherries, eating some and taking the rest home to crush and put into bottles, to which we added water to make our own drinks. Other times, depending on the season, we'd fill our socks with yellow plums, sand pears, or walnuts; or we'd spot and pick ears of dried corn, place them in an old burlap sack, and race home to make popcorn.

Mom did most of the cooking, and she was great at it. My sisters usually pitched in to assist her, but of the boys, I was most eager to help in the kitchen. I was fascinated with the way my mother could take multiple plain ingredients and make something delicious out of them. Her corn bread, turnip greens, and sweet potato pies were mouthwatering, and one of my favorite things to help her prepare was macaroni and cheese. She usually made enough to fill several large casserole dishes, sometimes allowing me to scoop and spread the mixture. Adding cheese slices between layers and on top was exciting, and I looked forward to the final touch: sprinkling dried parsley. While it baked, a comforting, cozy aroma filled the air, and I could hardly wait to eat a corner serving with burned cheese around the edges. However, I enjoyed making biscuits the best because they required few ingredients, were fun to cut out, and cooked so quickly. My dad had brought home an old sheet pan, formerly used in a school cafeteria; the item looked as big as a surfboard, which shows how many biscuits my mother normally made. But it wouldn't even fit in our oven. Therefore, Dad cut the cooking sheet in half using a hacksaw. Mom and I would grease both halves of the pan, place cut-out biscuit dough on top, and clean up as the biscuits baked. Hot, fluffy, and golden brown from the oven, I'd brush the biscuits with butter, and Mom would let me test our creations. They were delicious!

I think my dad could find a fishing hole anywhere. Time and again, he'd put on old rubber boots and trudge through the woods, sometimes for thirty or forty minutes, until he located a pond or creek. In tow was his cane pole, complete with a hook and a plastic bottle cap for a cork. His bait bucket was a small, rusted tin can that he had poked holes in on both sides near the top, then ran part of a wire clothes hanger through for a handle. He'd layer the can with black soil and earthworms he dug up outside. In addition, he always carried a homespun fish stringer shaped from a flexible metal coat hanger, which he straightened, then bent into the shape of hooks on both ends, and threaded through the gills of the bream, catfish, pinfish, and mullet he caught. That was how he brought home his catch. After cleaning and deboning were finished, he usually cooked a large pot of fish soup with corn and potatoes. He also made "corn flitters" to go with it. Dad blended his own cornmeal from dried corn in a used mixer, combined the cornmeal with eggs, and dropped the mixture into a pan of hot grease to fry. "Flitters" were a family favorite.

My parents were on the same sheet of music when it came to raising my siblings and me. My mother wrote chore charts every week and oversaw all indoor tasks, and my father made sure we took care of outdoor chores.

Assignments rotated, and boys and girls alike had to wash and dry dishes and mow the lawn using the second-hand manual push mower we owned at the time. If we missed an area of grass in the yard or we didn't make the beds properly, we had to go back and fix our mistake; we were taught not to do just enough to get by, but to do things right. Even very young children were given damp rags to clean windowsills or assigned to empty small trashcans, sweep, or perform other basic tasks.

Although my parents agreed on how to raise us, when it came to education they had different teaching methods. My mother was traditional, pushing bookwork, and my father was more hands-on and practical.

My father would give my siblings and me packages of seeds and tell us, "You need to know the name of what you're planting because some things grow differently." He'd ask us to read and spell the names on the packages. Those who pronounced words correctly and got letters right were sometimes rewarded with a nickel, which was valuable since we could buy windmill cookies for a penny from the local convenience store. When my father asked us to count ripe red tomatoes, they stood out like light bulbs on a stalk. Whoever made it back first with the correct answer was the winner. Sometimes he'd quiz us: "What's one squash plus three squash?" Other times he'd ask, "If you have ten potatoes, your brother eats two, and your sister eats one, how many are left?"

Both of my parents were old school and believed in physical punishment. That was the way they were taught. However, they did emphasize it was done out of love and never meanness or lack of control. If adults were talking, my siblings and I were not to hang around like bees guarding honey or interrupt unless there was an emergency. If we were outside playing in the yard, we had to be inside by sundown and were not allowed to go to friends' houses until we reached a specific age. Once we came in for the evening and bathed, my parents made us wear every-day clothes for sleeping. They enforced respect from the beginning.

We all knew the rules. At seven-thirty in the evening, we'd gather in the living room, and sometimes Mom or Dad would say a short prayer; then we'd take turns using the one bathroom we had to brush our teeth and shower. The girls went first, then the boys—oldest to youngest. Those of us waiting our turn watched the old-fashioned RCA TV in the living room, with aluminum foil on the antennas to bring in the picture a little clearer; it was the only television in the house. Two of my favorite shows were *Lawrence Welk* and *The Donny and Marie Osmond Show*. However, those weren't very popular with my siblings, and I was usually outvoted to watch *Good Times* or *Walking Tall*. As I got older I also liked *Gilligan's Island*, *Dukes of Hazzard*, and *Love Boat*. At nine o'clock my sisters proceeded to their bedroom and my brothers and

I went to ours. We would make our way to the bunk beds lining the walls and either roll or dive onto the bottom bunks or scamper up wooden ladders to the top, like squirrels heading up a tree. The cheap ladders that came with the aging bunk bed sets continually broke, so my father made sturdier ones to use. Some of us didn't have beds; therefore, we slept on cots or palates of blankets on the floor, depending on our ages.

My mother emphasized God was always with us when no one else was. I even stumbled upon my dad praying by himself a couple of times. Once, I was asked to retrieve Mom's purse from her bedroom where I noticed a huge white book on the dresser. On the front cover was a picture of a man with a halo above his head, and when I lifted the cover to peek inside, boy, was I in for a surprise! The letters were so big and fancy; their dips and curls were scattering all over the pages, like ants trying to find their way. As I flipped through, I realized the book was a Bible, and it was interspersed with birth certificates and newspaper clippings. Even though my family attended church in the early years, I never recall going until I was an adult. At a point, it became a financial challenge for my parents. If my family had been more like the Flintstones, at least gasoline wouldn't have been a problem: we had sixteen horsepower!

Chapter Two

Growing up, all of my brothers and sisters seemed very intelligent, but I wasn't. While in first grade, I realized I was different. The teacher asked all of the students to recall a story about their summer, but I would lose my train of thought and couldn't finish. That pattern continued throughout elementary school and led to me being picked on and even beaten up. At least twice on the school bus, the same bully punched me in the face. One time when my older sister found out, she drew back her fists and gave him a couple of "knuckle sandwiches"—and it wasn't even lunchtime!

I remember being called on in class to read or spell a word. I would feel myself panic. I tried to remain in control, but frequently my heart would speed up, I'd break into a cold sweat and start to shake. Students would die laughing at me, as if they were viewing an episode of *The Three Stooges*. At times, I honestly thought I was going to pass out. Often, I'd ask the teacher if I could be dismissed to the bathroom, or I'd simply run out of class and go there to try to calm myself down.

I recall escaping to the restroom one time, glancing into the mirror, and seeing my reflection as I sobbed. I realized something was really wrong with me. I wondered, *Why can't I be normal?*

I decided I'd ask my parents why I couldn't focus or learn as well as my classmates who were the same age. They told me all kids learn at different rates, but it would come. "Just worry about yourself, and I'll help you," Mom insisted. She would call out words, encouraging me to memorize the letters, and she followed along in books while I tried to pronounce and understand what I was reading. In spite of her efforts, I would lose my focus, and the information wouldn't sink in. "You're not trying hard enough!" Mom would yell. It was then I realized I was being chased by the Ghost of Inability to Learn.

During elementary school, I remember being called to the front of the classroom to solve the math problem "3x3." I shyly made my way to the chalkboard, and was glued there because the 3s looked like Es. While I stood in a trance, my classmates giggled and attempted to contain their laughter. *If I could only turn into a butterfly, I could take flight and free myself,* I thought. My teacher tried to assist me with the math problem, and I sensed she wished she could help with my learning problem, but she couldn't.

Later that day, when my class went to the playground, a little boy came up to me and announced, "My dad said the reason you're stupid is because you're black!" I thought about his comment, but was confused since my brothers and sisters were black too and all of them could read, write, and use numbers. I never told my family how I was treated at school, because I was afraid they would use that against me.

At the time, I don't think even the teachers within the local school system understood why I had learning issues. In their minds, I just wasn't applying myself, and that's what they told my parents, who in turn passed the information on to me. Due to a lack of knowledge, my educators' conclusions confirmed what Mom and Dad had already assumed, and as a result, my parents pushed me until I almost broke. They implemented punishment because they wanted me to be as smart as my siblings.

Once, Mom smacked me on the side of the head and said, "Maybe I can knock some sense in there." Then she went in my room and took my worn-out basketball, soccer ball, or whatever used toys I valued, and said I'd get them back when I started making better grades. I cried, but it didn't change anything. At times, my parents would also reduce food as punishment because I couldn't learn the school material to their satisfaction. Other times, they would try to motivate me to learn. "Don't you know if you get an education, you could be the next president?" Mom would urge. I understood what was expected of me and tried even harder.

Eventually I came up with the idea to write two-letter words on paper, slice them down the middle like a piece of pie, and hide them in the house. I would then go into another room, count to twenty, and come out searching for the letters. Once they were located, I put them together to sound out the word. The activity not only improved my pronunciation but my spelling and memory as well, and over time I pushed myself to learn five-letter words. My sisters and brothers thought it looked like a fun game, so they started helping me hide and find letters, which made me feel better about myself. In addition, I prayed every night for God to give me magical powers so I could be smarter.

Typically, I would sit at the dining table after school, alongside my brothers and sisters, and try to do homework. Mom was usually in the kitchen cooking at that time of day, and my mind would frequently drift onto what she was doing. She never used a cookbook or recipe, and I remember thinking cooking seemed pretty simple compared to what I was doing. It was as if someone had flipped a switch and a light came on. *Maybe I can be a cook one day*, I imagined. *I would get two for one: I'd have a job and be around food, so I'd always be able to eat.*

Afternoons often turned into evenings as I remained at the dining table, trying to write and practice spelling words. Sometimes I stayed up all night long and still never got them. When copying words, the letters seemed to dance around on the paper and never be still, resembling my childhood idol, Michael Jackson—gliding forward and moonwalking backward, as if he had the moon underneath his feet.

My spelling tests were on Fridays, and I dreaded them with a passion. I would get quite nervous the night before because I knew I was going to fail the test and then be punished. It got to the point where I was so scared my fear caused me to wet the bed; therefore, I would wake up early and try to change the sheets before I got in trouble for that too. Sure enough, when I'd bring home a bad grade on my spelling test, I would get a whipping with a belt or a drop cord, and believe me, it hurt. But I thought I deserved it. I also wouldn't be allowed to go outside and play all weekend, and my meal portions would be reduced. I would often sneak back into the kitchen after everyone was asleep, searching for more food. Many times there was none to be found.

In fact, as our family grew, there were never too many groceries in the house. I even noticed my parents missing a meal or two, and once asked an older brother, "Why didn't

Mom and Dad eat tonight?" With a disturbed look on his face, he hesitated. "To be so young, you sure are a curious one." Not settling for that as an answer, I asked again, and my brother whispered, as if we were secret agents, "You didn't hear it from me, but sometimes there's not enough to go around. Mom and Dad often go without a lot of things just for us. One day you'll understand."

Had it been up to my parents' desires, everyone in our family would have been allowed to consume anything, anytime, as long as it wasn't junk food; but our options depended on whether or not our garden was in season and when and how much Dad got paid. Many times, Mom would can vegetables we grew to save for leaner times, but we'd eventually run out of them, as we would the groceries my parents purchased. My siblings and I would have thought we'd found a pot of gold if we had ever been offered three meals a day; that was merely a dream. If we were lucky, we'd get one meal or just a snack, and some days nothing. Even when I wasn't being punished, I remember being so hungry I would cry until my mouth was dry, and I'd wake up hoarse the next day. Often I'd gather my brothers and sisters outside, and we'd stand in a circle holding hands as I prayed for food. Many times, I'd walk around and see neighbors with their curtains open eating a meal and wish I were them.

Chapter Three

Even if food was in the house, my parents didn't always have a way to cook it because sometimes there was no money to fill the gas tank to run our gas stove. On occasion, if there was cheese and bread in the kitchen, Mom would give each child a sandwich. To doctor mine up, I would sneak the iron, plug it in, and press the outside pieces of bread to create a grilled cheese sandwich. However, when there were no prize ingredients, as was often the case, I'd ingest plain flour or mix it with lard or eat crunchy dried rice—whatever I could find. Unlike Dr. Seuss's "Sam-I-am," I would have gladly eaten "*green eggs and ham.*"

Our family had a heater that ran on gas too, and there were times I would shiver and shake until I thought I would turn into a human Popsicle. When my brothers, sisters, and I saw the gasman show up to fill the tank, it was like Christmas; we knew our parents would be able to prepare hot food and we'd all stay warm, at least for a little while.

Eventually, Dad built a fireplace with a nice brick chimney and inserted a wood-burning stove as a backup for cooking and to keep our family warm during winter. It was great as long as we had plenty of firewood, but sometimes we ran out and had to venture into nature's cold, frosty hug to locate and chop more. My parents would use the wood-burning stove year-round to cook, and in the summer the house would get extremely hot. We had no air-conditioning, and at times our electricity was disconnected due to lack of payment, so we couldn't even turn on a fan.

My father owned an old, faded, run-down Chevrolet station wagon. Often it would fail to run, leaving him stranded. I think he had every Ace bandage and Band-Aid in the county on it. At times the car would sit in our driveway for months until he could scrape up the money for repairs. Acquaintances would tell Dad they'd drive him into town to get parts to fix the car, or they'd agree to give him a ride back from the mechanic's shop, but many times they didn't follow through. And if they did show up, they charged him an arm and a leg. Therefore, my father learned to depend on himself when it came to getting from point A to point B.

Dad's job was prepping and painting vehicles at an auto body shop. Many times, if his car was on the blink or he didn't have gas money, he'd wake up early to start the long trek into Jacksonville to work. On average it took over three hours, depending on the weather. Dad would typically make his way down our driveway onto the long, straight dirt road leading from the house onto the paved road. He'd continue heading toward Jacksonville the whole time, and if he was lucky, he'd successfully thumb a ride. But sometimes he was only able to catch a ride part of the way, so he'd walk the rest. He followed a similar routine when returning home. However, more times than not he had to depend on his own two feet and his sheer desire to support his family.

Consequently, during warmer months, it wasn't unusual to see Dad's work boots kicking up gray dust along our black dirt driveway as he made his way into or back from town. And during winter, my siblings and I would watch from the windows as his footprints left a trail in the snow. As soon as we caught a glimpse of Dad walking home from work, we'd race down the driveway; you'd think we were in an African-American Olympics and Dad was the finish line. We wanted to be the first to see if he had any food left in his metal Aladdin lunchbox.

My mother didn't have a driver's license. She

depended on my father to take her into town to get groceries. And sometimes when the car broke down or my parents didn't have money for gasoline, relatives would agree to give Mom a ride to a grocery store. But just like steam in a pot, something would often arise in their lives and they wouldn't be able to follow through. At times, this caused our family to go without food, but other times it was as if my parents were acting out the *Star Trek* theme song: they would seek out new ways. As children, we didn't ask questions; we were just happy to have a meal.

When I was in fourth grade, my siblings and I happened to be off from school one Friday and the weather was beautiful, so we spent the day running and playing outside in the yard. By afternoon we were famished and rushed into the kitchen like cowboys and Indians scouting for food. One of my siblings asked, "What can we eat, Mom?" With a sad look on her face, as if she'd lost her best friend, Mom replied, "It's going to be air puddin' tonight. Your dad doesn't get paid until tomorrow." Although we were disappointed, there was nothing we could do, so my younger brothers, sisters, and I walked around and pretended to bite and swallow big gulps of air —"air puddin'." We laughed at each other because we looked like fish out of water.

The main reason I looked forward to school was to eat; I dreaded the lack of food during holidays and school breaks. Even though my parents brought food into the home, it seemed there was never enough. At one point in elementary school, I wanted to hide in the cafeteria. I thought when the doors were locked, I could eat all I wanted and stay warm at night, too. Although I never did it, the idea made me feel better.

Chapter Four

O nce, after I'd had an unusually stressful day at school, my siblings and I caught the bus home, as we normally did. We made our way down the dirt road to our driveway, walked up the steps, and when we opened the front door, Dad was home. He never made it home before we did, but this time he had and was holding a couple of full large trash bags in his hands. The biggest smile spread across his face from ear to ear, like Obama's the day he won the presidency. Dad told us to come on over and look through the bags to see if there was anything we wanted. I perked up right away, ready to dive in, as if bobbing for apples. The sound of rustling plastic bags filled the living room, and a few minutes later, I raised my head from one of the sacks and was holding a small silver electronic device called a Walkman. After studying the device to figure out how it worked, I saw it was missing batteries, so I borrowed some from a nearby clock. As I heard the radio play through the attached earmuff-style headset, I bounced with excitement. What a find!

Leaving my siblings to claim the remaining items, I clipped my prize Walkman to the side of my jeans and made my way outside across the yard onto a nearby wooded nature trail. It was a beautiful autumn afternoon as my feet plowed through the red, orange, yellow, and brown leaves. At the end of the pathway was a half-cropped cornfield I had visited countless times after challenging days at school. My ritual was to fall to my knees there, stare at the sun, and pray. This time was no exception. I pulled off the headset, dropped to my knees, and stared up at the sun as tears streamed down my face. I started praying, begging God for another brain or for magical powers to use the one I had. As I gathered myself and rose to my feet, planning to return home, I placed the headset back over my ears. On the spot, one of my favorite Jackson 5 songs played on the Walkman, and I found myself stirring to move to the music. Feeling the beat of the instruments, my head bobbed up and down like a cork in the water, as if a fish were tugging at it. My body began swaying, and suddenly I found myself spinning, skipping, and leaping across the vastness of the cornfield. It was a wonderful feeling. That was when I first learned of one of the gifts God had given me—the gift of dancing. Over the years, I continued to frequent the cornfield with the Walkman, get on my knees, stare at the sun, pray, then dance and dance. I felt so free. But dancing was only a temporary escape from my problems.

As a fifth grader, I remember getting an excruciating toothache one weekend. The throbbing pain started in my left jaw, then radiated throughout my head; tears spilled from my eyes and rolled down my cheeks. However, my parents couldn't afford to take me to the dentist. They gave me medication, but it didn't help. I was so miserable one night that I couldn't sleep and began rocking back and forth in the bed. As the torment intensified, I started banging my head on the wall, trying to distract myself from my suffering. As the agony increased, so did my head banging, and I ended up making a hole in the drywall.

That Monday I went to school, and the pounding pain persisted. I tried not to cry but couldn't help it. When my teacher saw me, she sent me to the main office with a note requesting the school nurse take a look at me. The cafeteria supervisor happened to be standing nearby and overheard the nurse tell me my jaw was swollen and inflamed and I needed to go to the dentist right away. Since there was no one to take me, the woman in charge of the cafeteria was kind enough to volunteer. She called my mother to explain there was an emergency and assured Mom it would not cost her anything. Mom agreed, and I was taken to the dentist. The cafeteria supervisor paid for my treatment herself. I was so grateful; I offered to wash her car as repayment, but she said that wasn't necessary. Afterwards, she drove me home.

The next day, just before school was out, I stopped by the lunchroom to thank the supervisor again, and she gave me forty cents and a couple of sandwiches. I think, having seen my large family and where I lived the day before, she realized how poor we were and how much I needed the help. Plus, I was as skinny as a toothpick. From then on I would stop by the cafeteria about twenty minutes before the final bell. Sometimes the supervisor would give me a little change—ten cents, thirty cents—and she'd often give me leftover food. She was a godsend.

Chapter Five

Any coins I was given or earned I kept inside a sock, hidden first by wedging it up into the wooden slats of a box spring and later by lifting a lightweight nightstand and shoving the sock into the hollow underneath. All the while, my mind visualized Blow Pops, Mary Janes, Sugar Daddies, and other goodies I could buy from the neighborhood country convenience store if I saved enough money.

To earn more, one of my brothers and I decided to collect used glass Coke and Pepsi bottles because there was a five-cent refund for each one. We didn't have many bottles at home, so we'd look around the neighborhood, in the woods, or ask our uncles who visited if they had any in their cars. Sometimes we gathered enough bottles to fill every square hole in a wooden beverage crate Dad had brought home. My brother would grab one side of the crate and I'd take hold of the other as we happily jaunted eight to ten minutes to the little convenience store to turn in our collection. The shop owner would count our returns and hand my brother the refund, which he always split with me. When our other siblings realized what we were doing, they wanted in on the action and would follow us, often snatching up bottles before we could. Hence, my brother and I came up with a secret code. "We're going to look for submarines," we said. After all, when a bottle was tipped on its side, it looked like a submarine. "Operation Submarine" was a success and kept the others from trailing so closely, leaving us time to locate our prized glass treasures.

Another time, at age eleven, I remember walking to the country store with my brother. We arrived, pushed the metal handle to open the glass door, and wandered around inside the cement-block building as though we were mice in a maze. We gazed at snacks until we both picked out items to buy. I had chosen a small package of cookies but couldn't read the name of them because the letters seemed to spin around like a cartoon character. As I examined the writing, my brother placed his selection on the counter and counted out his money perfectly. Then it was my turn. When I stepped up to pay, the store owner told me my total, but I wasn't able to add up my money. Feeling very nervous, I emptied my pockets, placed all of my coins on the counter, and pushed them toward the man. As I turned to walk away, he remarked, "A stupid nigger—at that age, can't even count his own money!" My brother heard the man's words and said he was telling Dad, but I told him I didn't want the store owner to get in trouble. I knew I was dumb; some of my family members had told me I was. I thought, *What is the difference between the owner of the store and those family members?* There was no real difference.

I was well aware of my lack of ability and, as a seventh grader, it was called to the attention of others when I was frequently asked to read aloud in social studies. I would try my best to pronounce the words but was often interrupted by classmates' snickering and whispering as I forged ahead. Once, when called on to read, I simply refused by remaining quiet. Not knowing what the punishment would be, I assumed I could handle it better than further humiliation by my schoolmates. The teacher put class on hold, pulled a long wooden paddle out of his desk drawer, and walked me outside. "When you don't know something, it's my job to assist you. You must participate in class!" he stated. Then he summoned another teacher to witness, which was school policy, as he had me bend over and touch my knees while he administered two strong whacks across my backside. I sensed the teacher wanted to let me off but couldn't or other students might behave in a similar manner. I knew I was wrong.

That was my first paddling in school, but not the last. A few others came when I was still in seventh grade after failing spelling tests and being told by the teacher to write each misspelled word up to one hundred times each. If I was close to completing the task, I was in the clear, but if not, I was in for a paddling.

At twelve or thirteen years old, I got fed up with myself one night, while up late studying long after my family was asleep. With tears rolling down my cheeks, I gathered some clothes and a blanket, stuffed them into a pillowcase, and dashed out of the house toward the woods, as if a wolf were chasing me. I had a small, old flashlight but dropped it. Reaching down, I fumbled to retrieve it and couldn't get it to work. As I lifted my head, lightning bugs filled the air and landed on tree branches, illuminating my way, as though they were awaiting my arrival—the most beautiful thing I'd ever seen! Uneasy, yet mesmerized by so many lightning bugs, I crept into the woods and curled up at the base of a young oak tree with the blanket I'd packed. I tried to fall asleep, but wild sounds kept me on edge. A loud roar echoed throughout the woods, and I shivered and gripped the tree tightly—you would have thought Bigfoot was being unleashed! An owl and whippoorwill seemed to converse all night long. It was as if the owl would ask, "*Who* is in the woods?" And the whippoorwill would answer. The breaking of branches and rustling of leaves on the ground sounded like a stampede coming toward me, and I raised my head to catch a glimpse of four deer trotting by as lightning bugs followed. However, as I lay there, the enchanting glow of the lightning bugs grew dim, and reality set in.

Early the next morning before sunrise, I returned home. The windows of the house were locked with sticks, as they usually were at night; therefore, I couldn't push them open. I had to use the front door. So I timidly knocked. Mom was already up, checking to see if I was at the table from the night before, still trying to learn. When she met me at the door, she seemed mysterious and concerned as she tugged at the pillowcase of clothes and the blanket slung over my back. "You can't run away from your problems. Running away doesn't solve anything," she advised. Then she pulled out a belt and gave me a stern whipping; afterwards, she hugged me and sent me to bed.

At home, when my siblings and I weren't doing chores or studying, we preferred to be outside—especially me. However, I dreaded the sight, sound, or feel of rain. It meant we all had to be in the house, and a couple of my siblings enjoyed picking on me, as brothers and sisters typically do. My poor performance in school didn't help the situation either. It seemed they were coyotes and I was the Road Runner, so when they targeted me, I tried to avoid them as much as possible, which was difficult. I knew they didn't mean any harm, but I still didn't like the teasing. Often I'd find myself standing outside under the overhang of the roof, wishing for the rain to stop, and hoping my parents didn't notice I wasn't indoors with the others.

As the number of my siblings continued to rise, my father eventually added another bedroom to our home, for a total of five. He would usually start building around tax season after receiving a refund and then borrow more money from a credit union, which took installments from his paychecks. I don't know where Dad got his knowledge to build, but he did quality work. He was truly a jack-of-all-trades. When I saw him toting two-by-fours over his shoulders and climbing up the ladder, he reminded me of a beaver building its dam—he was on a mission! Those of us kids old enough to use a hammer and nails would assist with construction. My brothers and I would sometimes slip and smash our own fingers and thumbs, but that didn't stop us. We knew quitting wasn't an option; my father would punish us if we tried to avoid helping. He believed if we had energy to run around outside and play, the same could be used to help the family.

While working on the room addition, Dad would increasingly single me out. Knowing I didn't excel in school, he had me count the steps on the ladder and spell out l-a-d-d-e-r. He would throw me a tape measure, asking exactly how many feet and inches were in a board's length or width. If my siblings tried to answer before I did, Dad would usually stop them. Sometimes he'd send me to the shed to read the nail boxes and retrieve a specific number of one- or two-inch penny nails or roofing nails. He would add, "On your way back, memorize the letters so you can spell the words when you return." If I was successful, he was pleased. If not, while my siblings played or watched TV, I had to practice counting or spelling the words I had missed. Dad eventually gave me my own tape measure, and I was as happy as a lark. He'd give me small pieces of scrap wood and have me learn to read their measurements. If he quizzed me a couple of days later and I couldn't answer correctly, I'd see the expression on his face and think, *Oh boy, I'm in trouble!*

Once construction was completed, my parents re-orchestrated our room assignments: boys' rooms were on one side of the house, and girls' were on the other. And with every project my father and I worked on together, he continued to keep me on my toes. Looking back, I now realize that I learned quite a bit about a tape measure— enough to build a house to keep me out of the weather if I had to.

Chapter Six

When I was thirteen and out of school on summer vacation, I landed my first job for pay. Like my older brothers before me, I cut grass for a lady and her parents. Twice a week, sure as clockwork, the lady would drive to our home and I'd hop in back of her truck, riding to the locations where she provided a push mower, weed-eater, and gasoline. When I began, I was so thin and small she asked if I was certain I could do the job. I assured her I could and placed my foot on top of the push mower as I yanked the handle to the cord to crank the engine. The motor sounded similar to an airplane propeller ready for takeoff, but I didn't mind; visions of cool new school clothes flashed before my eyes as I daydreamed about getting paid. "You must know what you're doing," the woman concluded before retreating indoors, out of the heat, to let me work. Because her yard was probably a couple of acres, it seemed as soon as I forced the lawnmower through the tall grass, I'd look behind me and fresh green grass would sprout back up like a porcupine. It took most of a day to complete the job, but "little ol' me" just kept on going.

On the other hand, I could finish her parents' yard in under two hours but would often stay longer completing extra outdoor tasks her mother requested of me. The first day, the lady who had hired me commented that I had finished quicker than some who had previously mowed using a riding mower, which left me feeling pretty good until I found out I would be paid $3.35 per hour. Initially, I went along with it, but the next day I told her I didn't think the pay was enough. She then offered to compensate me twenty-five dollars for her yard and fifteen for her mother's. "I think twenty-five for each yard would be better," I said. She gasped and replied, "I've never paid that much before! Let me speak to my mother." She walked inside, and I overheard her mother through the kitchen window. "I like the way he does extra things around here. He's a nice kid," she explained. The next thing I knew, my employer had emerged with good news. "Okay, I will pay you twenty-five dollars for each yard," she agreed. I was elated and realized it really *paid* to speak up for myself on the job.

My older brothers couldn't believe the deal I had

worked, and my mother thought I was joking. "How did you manage that?" she asked. "That's a big yard, Mom, so I asked for more," I plainly said. "That's the first step in taking up for yourself when it comes to work," she replied. So twice a week, tired, dirty, and hungry, I bounced up our steps, went inside, and handed over my earnings to Mom, as all of my working siblings did. She kept the majority to spend on bills and groceries and left me with a little to buy goodies at the country store. Originally, I was sad to see my hard-earned cash quickly disappear, but I knew it was to help us all.

The following summer I cut grass again, while my eldest brothers worked for a local tobacco farmer. When I happened to catch sight of one of their weekly paychecks for $186, I wanted to know how soon I could join them. "It's no treat working in that hot sun all day. Are you sure you want to work on a farm?" one of my brothers asked. I had no doubt. "Yes!" I replied. So the plan was for me to work in the tobacco fields the next summer, when I was fifteen. I could hardly wait for the time to arrive, and as it neared, I grew more enthusiastic.

Finally the big day came. Two of my older brothers and I woke up early to get ready. I put on jeans, tennis shoes, a long-sleeve shirt, and a baseball cap, and before sunup, we walked from our driveway down the dirt road to the paved street. Shortly thereafter, a pickup truck stopped, and we piled in back with other men and women headed to the field. After taking one look at me, workers' whispers sounded like a swarm of bees hovering above, and one woman commented to a man, "You know that skinny baby needs to stay home!" Then they and other field hands had a hearty laugh at my expense.

I was unfazed by the comment, and when we arrived at our destination, I sprang from the bed of the vehicle. I could see rows of green tobacco for days. One of my brothers had agreed to take me under his wing and show me the ropes of pulling tobacco, so I felt confident it was going to be a great day. I was amazed at the size of some of the leaves; I could have probably used one as a canoe to float downstream!

True to his word, my brother showed me how to break the giant leaves at the base of the stalk first and work my way up, flapping them under my arm to secure them. He then walked further up the row, leaving me to my task. I noticed leaves at the bottom of the stalk weighed more due to dirt splashing on them from previous rain, and all were currently wet with dew. As I clenched to hold them in place, they not only grew heavier but also soaked my clothing. I piled more and more under my arm until I looked down and saw something frightening on one of the leaves. I immediately jumped, flailing my arms and legs in the air, dropping every single leaf I'd gathered, and took off running, full speed ahead, down the row toward my brother. My legs were moving so quickly I was kicking my backside with the back of my heels. Huffing and puffing, I tugged at my brother's sleeve. "There's a fat, little green snake on one of the leaves! Come look!" I yelled. "It's got a lot of legs!" I added. My brother burst out laughing, clutched his side, and fell to the ground; his howling laughter could be heard throughout the rows. "You silly thing! There's no snake that short. It's only a tobacco worm," he chuckled.

I reluctantly went back to my post but changed my method to begin pulling the crop from the top so I could see any "creepy crawlies" before they saw me. My energy waned as the sun sent down its rays of penetrating heat, yet I continued to gather and throw the giant leaves into a wagon attached to a tractor that periodically drove down the rows. If the tractor hadn't returned from the barn yet, other workers and I would form large heaps of leaves and hoist them into the wagon when it returned. And those pesky green worms were everywhere!

By the end of day one, I absolutely hated the job with a passion! I planned to warn my younger brothers and sisters to NEVER work in tobacco, and I didn't want to return the following day either. But I thought of the way my father had done things he probably didn't like in order to support our family. So the next day I was back to it—just more prepared. From then on, I wore two long-sleeve shirts, two pairs of pants, and a pair of gloves so I wouldn't have to feel the worms between my fingers. I also wore a rag over my head and a large round-brimmed hat.

Picking tobacco as a kid was one of the hardest jobs I ever had. Mondays through Fridays and sometimes Saturdays were spent in the field. Work began at 6:00 a.m. and I'd get drenched from the cumbersome dew-soaked leaves. By noon, as the sun radiated creating a sauna effect, I felt like a human clothesline. When it rained, I continued to work; otherwise, I wouldn't be paid. But sometimes, if the weather was severe, I'd slip and slide into the bed of a truck that transported me, along with other workers, to the shelter of a tent. However, we sometimes had to continue working in the conditions for up to an hour before a vehicle was free from the barn to retrieve us. By day's end, I was always dirty as well as sticky from the thick liquid that oozed from the plants, to say nothing of my encounters with insects and hornworms.

At the end of that season, my parents bought me some school shirts and a beautiful pair of shiny white tennis shoes, which I cleaned every day for over thirty days! Even though I despised working in tobacco, the new clothes, especially the shoes, motivated me to forge ahead. I felt like I was in the movie *Rocky*—I was ready for another round.

At sixteen, I started the summer laboring in the sweltering heat again. By that time, a few things had changed on the farm, including the loading process of tobacco leaves. Once gathered, I'd force the foliage onto metal prongs emerging from each side of a rectangular rack. Other workers would then close the receptacles and load them in back of an industrial-size truck to be transported to the barn.

One day, much to my surprise, the farmer came to my row and asked if I'd like to transfer to the barn. I leaped at the opportunity. "Yes, I would!" I replied, as thoughts of shade and lower temperatures flowed through my mind. My new task was to unload racks of tobacco from a truck and heave them into ovens to cook. When the racks cooled, a timer buzzed, signaling me to remove and empty their brown contents into huge burlap sacks that I loaded onto the bed of another vehicle. The job involved a lot of lifting, but I viewed it as a workout; I was killing two birds with one stone, so to speak. On occasion I'd encounter a green worm but—thankfully—not nearly the gobs I'd seen in the field.

Eight-hour days called for a short break or two, so the four or five other barn workers and I would briefly make small talk. "Thank goodness we're working in here," a coworker commented one afternoon. I nodded in agreement. "Although I love my color, it is roasting out there and I don't miss working on my tan," I stated. They cracked up, and I laughed too.

Even though working in the barn was better than toiling in the field, I still detested working in tobacco.

What I learned from it was, sometimes, as a law-abiding citizen, you have to do things you don't want to do for the sake of yourself and others.

When the following June rolled around, I was ready to turn over a new leaf—and not one on a tobacco stalk! So I applied to wash dishes at a very popular seafood restaurant in the neighboring town of Cape Carteret. I was hired, and the place was hopping every night of the week. I usually caught a ride there, but my goal was to save enough to purchase my own vehicle. Therefore, I remained employed year round until high school graduation.

One evening when I was in the kitchen prepping the dishwasher, I overheard that the eatery was short busboys. I was told to fill in, so I did. At the start of the next shift, in front of my coworkers, I was asked to try my hand at being a short-order cook. I agreed to give it a shot, and cooking wasn't a problem. However, deciphering handwritten orders from various waiters and waitresses proved to be a challenge. Unlike today, no abbreviations were used, such as SW meaning "steak well done." All orders were fully written out, sometimes quickly and unclearly. Figuring out how to slow print down on paper was hard enough, let alone dealing with cursive writing; to me, it resembled people joined together in a three-legged sack race. Sometimes there were as many as thirty tickets on the counter, and the lead cook would ask me to read orders aloud to speed things up, which rattled my nerves. I winged it for two nights, but the pressure got to me, and I think the manager realized I had difficulty reading.

Following the second night of trying to make heads or tails of the written orders, I spoke to the manager after closing and requested that I be allowed to go back to busing tables. He initially hesitated but went on to explain how the owner and his family had been dining in-house the night I had bused tables and had been amazed at how fast I was. "The owner figured if you're that quick at busing tables and loading and unloading the dishwasher, you'd make a great short-order cook," he continued. I appreciated the compliment, but I was much more comfortable being a busboy. Plus, I already had down my method to fill the bus tub: silverware first, followed by plates, bowls, and glasses. Because I was shortchanged when it came to certain abilities, my mind developed systems for handling things.

Another great aspect of busing was that the waiters and waitresses shared tips with me, and before long, I had enough money to purchase a used Pontiac T-1000! I was as happy as the day I had gotten my new pair of white tennis shoes, and I babied my car even more.

Chapter Seven

A round the time I made it into high school, I hit a growth spurt and decided to add workouts to my schedule, like my big brothers had. At home, we didn't have access to free weights or workout machines, so we'd attach one-gallon milk jugs filled with water to each end of a broomstick or fill old pillowcases or sacks with dirt and tie a couple to the ends of branches to be lifted or curled. I thought life would be easier on campus since I was bigger and could defend myself. However, I was in for a rude awakening.

When I entered ninth grade, I found out I was going to be in six regular classes and one special education class. I could no longer hide among the other students. Special ed singled me out, and I was embarrassed, hurt, and ashamed. Every day that I could, I would enter special ed five minutes late and would always request to be excused to the restroom five minutes before class finished. That way, the likelihood of someone seeing me enter or exit the class would be less. If I happened to be talking to friends in the hall and they wouldn't leave, I would dart into the bathroom until the coast was clear, and then I'd go to my special ed class. (Yes, I had tardy slips up to Mount Everest.) Unfortunately, some people found out my secret and picked on me.

As high school progressed, I was placed in a second special education class. My peers would frequently ask what I was doing in those classes since I was fairly popular at school. I always tried to dodge their questions and bring up other subjects. At one point, while enrolled in special ed, I noticed more and more students staring at me. I thought they all knew my secret, and I felt like I was playing the role of Batman in the movie titled the same; I'd gone from being the good guy people liked to being the bad guy people questioned.

In several of my regular academic classes, I would break into a cold sweat and start shaking at times for fear the teacher would call on me. It wasn't that I couldn't do my work; I just wasn't as fast as my classmates. Many times I'd start out doing an assignment, but feeling the time crunch, I'd often resort to scribbling on my paper. That tactic worked until one day the science teacher told the class to trade papers and check each other's answers. I was in a state of shock, speechless, and felt a chill surge through my body, from the inside out, as if I'd swallowed a glass of ice cubes. I sensed I might pass out, and I couldn't catch my breath. I managed to gather my things and run out of the room. The Ghost of Inability to Learn was haunting me still.

The next day, I made sure to arrive early to explain to my teacher why I had dashed away so suddenly the day before. He understood. From then on, he would allow me to check my own classwork, but other students still had to trade. They would question the teacher and me about the new rule, but neither of us divulged the reason.

I only had one teacher who really picked on me about my level of education; that person was one of my carpentry teachers. In the classroom he was pretty ruthless. He would insult me in front of fellow students. And he wouldn't even check my papers; he'd simply crumple them into a ball and toss them into the trashcan right in front of me. He would call on me to solve problems he'd written on the board, knowing I never had the answers. My peers would giggle and snicker, and he would too. Then the teacher would say something like, "Maybe you can get this one," and he'd write "4 + 4." He and the other students would burst out laughing.

Other times, the instructor and I would pass each other in the hall and he would make sly comments, followed by chuckling, and I knew he was targeting me. In many instances, he would give me a compliment, such as "Nice outfit," but in the same breath add an insult: "Does that girl you were walking with know you can't put two and two together at times?" I believe the teacher was well aware I was in special education. His badgering made me realize my mother was right: after high school I should never let people know of my difficulties with reading and writing.

One day after the carpentry teacher humiliated me, I became so frustrated, but I wasn't sure if I was more upset with the teacher or myself. I recall feeling like an animal boxed in a corner, and I then realized sometimes one has to stand up for oneself. So after class I did. In a calm voice, I told the carpentry teacher, "If you do that to me once more, I will scrub your face on that concrete floor." Afterwards I felt horrible for saying that to him. I knew it wasn't kind, but it helped my situation. That was the start of me learning to stand up for myself. The teacher never apologized, but he never made fun of me again either, although he continued to throw my papers away at times.

As I reflected on my dealings with the carpentry teacher, I realized I should have reported his behavior to a counselor or principal instead of taking matters into my own hands. I also concluded, regardless of circumstances, an educator should never bully a student.

Meanwhile, some teachers were supportive. In fact, during my study hall, one helped me review material needed to get my driver's permit, and I was grateful. I also took the driver's manual home to study on my own, and for a full month I invested two to three hours each day into learning the material by heart. When it was time to put pencil to paper and test, I admit I was anxious yet relieved to learn there wasn't a time limit in which to complete it. It took me a while to go from question to question, but I realized it was everything I had diligently memorized. Upon completion, I handed my work to the man administering the permit exam and patiently sat in a chair, awaiting the results. Approaching me, he extended his right hand and announced, "Congratulations, young man! You passed." I sprang to my feet, and as we shook hands, his words soaked into my mind like a dry sponge under a running faucet. I felt the corners of my lips automatically expand upward and across my face, and I don't think I could have controlled my happiness if I'd tried. "One down and one to go!" I exclaimed. When I left the Department of Motor Vehicles that day, driver's permit in hand, I practically bounced out of the building as if I were kin to Tigger the tiger. When I shared the terrific news with members of my family, they were very happy for me.

Subsequently, I signed up and took driver's education in school, which gave me road experience. Although I couldn't afford a vehicle at that time, I borrowed one from a friend, went back to the DMV, passed the driving test, and was awarded a license. It was a great day, and I hadn't been nervous at all. I had always been good at hands-on tasks; it was bookwork that usually stumped me.

Afterwards, I thought about how I had been able to learn the driver's manual so well, yet spelling words and various school materials didn't always sink in. *Why was that the case?* Then I noticed the differences. At school and at home there was a lot of pressure from others to learn and perform well, and I had a limited amount of time in which to do so. However, the usual stressors had not been there when I was poring over the driver's manual. I had picked up the booklet at school and didn't tell my family right away because I wanted to surprise them, which enabled me to take in the material at my own pace. Even when the teacher assisted, there was no outside pressure because we worked in the instructor's room during planning period. Circumstances seemed to make a difference. Plus, I wasn't going to let the Ghost of Inability to Learn steer me in the wrong direction. I had to have some kind of control.

One year, I signed up for home economics, thinking it might be an easier class for me since I had grown up watching my mother cook and I was fascinated by it. Thanks to her, I knew my way around a kitchen. I also saw her sew everything from curtains to clothes. I had even seen her make wallpaper out of old sheets and cloth and use lace as a wallpaper border.

Home economics started out well, and I think the

teacher could tell I had a genuine interest in the curriculum. During the first few days, fellow students and I made chocolate chip cookies and Rice Krispies treats, and the processes were easy for me because I had watched and helped Mom cook many times before.

One day the class was asked to read recipes out loud, and I felt myself grow jittery as my turn approached. There was no way to camouflage my weakness in the area of reading. I began, but my voice was shaky and unsure, and I started to mispronounce words. Without hesitation, my teacher dove in to rescue me, like a Navy Seal saving the president. For example, if the word was *peanuts* and I said *peas*, she'd make light of what I said by stating, "It could be *peas*, couldn't it?" She'd often praise me even after correcting me. I found myself hoping the teacher would always be there so I wouldn't have to deal with a substitute.

Because of the teacher's behavior, the other students treated me well. Regularly, we would be asked to cook with partners. We had to take turns reading the recipes aloud as the other person added ingredients and followed the instructions. I would always try to partner with the same girl, and when the teacher came by to assess our recipe, I'd have my partner read the recipe and I would explain it.

As the class progressed, the deadline to pay our home ec. fees rapidly approached, and I grew concerned. I spoke to the teacher after class, feeling as if butterflies were landing in my stomach. "I don't have the money," I managed to utter, with an embarrassed look on my face. She replied, "If you sweep the classroom floor on Fridays, I'll pay you five dollars. Then you can pay your fee from the money you earn." I thanked her and showed up every Friday after class to sweep the floor. She paid me as she'd said she would. And even after I'd earned enough to cover my home ec. fee, she continued to hire me to sweep on Fridays.

A boy from my neighborhood peeked in the window of the home ec. room and saw me cooking. He enjoyed teasing me and tried to elicit others to make fun of me as well. In spite of his efforts, my schoolmates only commented about the wonderful aromas coming from the classroom kitchen, and they'd eagerly wait for me to pass out brownies or cookies I'd made that day. Students would often comment, "You can really cook!" When the same boy found out I was sweeping the classroom floor for money, he was like a kid with a boom box—he turned it up, announcing to everyone on the school bus that I was a "do boy." Some thought it was so funny, they were practically rolling in the aisles, but I merely stared out the window, daydreaming of how I was going to spend my little pocket money. Gradually the boy stopped taunting me and actually wanted to become my friend, but I didn't trust him enough for that.

Home economics was a comfort zone for me; it was a place where I could excel and let my light shine. In spite of doing just okay on written tests, I got an A on the cooking and sewing portion and passed the class.

Challenges continued throughout high school, and I had to figure out better ways to do things. As a result, I learned to let the teachers know my limitations the first day of classes and would ask them not to call me to the board or test my knowledge verbally by asking me questions. I would also ask my brothers and sisters to help me write legible papers and assist with math problems, and if they weren't busy, they would. Other times, when my siblings were preoccupied, they'd want something in return. Therefore, I'd offer to give them some of my change, do their chores, iron their jeans, or let my brothers wear a pair of my shoes they liked if they would help.

During my primary educational years, I recall being tested by two doctors, once in the later years of elementary school and once in high school. However, I was never given results of the testing, and according to my parents, they were not aware of any test results either.

As I got older, my parents expected me to be further along with my education, but my ability to learn wasn't progressing as quickly as I'd hoped. As a result, my home life became more difficult. After hearing my parents lecture and yell at me about studying, several siblings tried getting on to me in a similar manner, hoping to motivate me. But they only made me feel worse. At one point, a cousin caught wind of my parents giving me a hard time due to my inability to read and write well, and he spread the news like wildfire. Thereafter, he and others tried to bully me.

My only solace to deal with the challenges was to grab the Walkman I'd had for years, head down the nearby nature trail to the half-cropped cornfield, look to the heavens and pray, then focus on the songs coming from the speakers on the headset, just as I did throughout childhood. I'd hear and feel the beat of the music; it always awakened something inside, causing me to leave negative emotions behind and focus on the positive through the expression of dancing. One afternoon when I was in eleventh grade, I picked up my treasured Walkman and placed the headset over my ears. I turned the device on, expecting to hear popular radio tunes, but there was only silence. I changed the batteries but still couldn't get it to work; I think I had simply worn it out. With the unfortunate breaking of the Walkman, my dancing ceased; and as graduation neared, and especially afterwards, life became busy, so dancing became a thing of the past. I was looking toward the future.

As twelfth grade progressed, I knew I wouldn't get my diploma. In fact, I didn't show up to have my picture made for the yearbook because I didn't feel I deserved a place in the senior class. When the yearbooks came out, my friends wanted me to sign theirs. Initially panic set in, but then I came up with an escape tactic. I told them I'd do it later, after I had time to think about what I wanted to write. The excuse worked, and I avoided having to write in anyone's yearbook.

In June of 1986 it was time for my high school graduation. This is how much the Ghost of Inability to Learn had a hold of me: it not only manipulated me to think I wasn't smart enough to deserve a spot in the graduating class, but it had the audacity to convince me I shouldn't take part in my own graduation ceremony. I tried to persuade my parents to believe the same because I didn't want to risk being humiliated. But they claimed I would look back one day and wish I had attended. The only reason I went was because my mother insisted. I had to stand in front of a crowd of hundreds of people, walk across the stage, and listen to them clap as I pretended to receive a diploma, when in actuality I was only handed a certificate. Although most in the audience didn't know, my mother, brothers, and sisters knew. I felt like I was on trial in front of the world and had let my family down. My father didn't attend, and I thought it was because he was disappointed in me. Later I found out he had to work.

I remember my mom telling me I would not make it anywhere in the world because I was too dumb. In fact, she wanted me to remain in Stella my whole life. I knew she was concerned about me. Mom didn't think I could be successful on my own, and she convinced a couple of my brothers and sisters to believe that also. She told me, "No woman in her right mind is going to put up with a dumb man." She said if I ventured out, I'd have to keep my inabilities a secret because according to some people in society, I already had one strike against me by being black. She explained that people would unfairly judge me for that, and she added, "Being dumb is even worse!" I came to realize those were her attempts to protect and save me from the world as she knew it.

Chapter Eight

There were many jobs I wanted, but the fact that written tests were required took me out of the running from the start. My top career choice out of high school was to join the Marines, and I had the honor to speak with a recruiter. I was very physically fit and felt I'd have no problem passing the PT test. However, I wasn't confident about the first step: scoring well on the Armed Services Vocational Aptitude Battery, a timed placement test. I was also interested in being a cop or a child therapist, but my limitations held me back.

Aware of my confines, I took on jobs fairly close to home. I was first hired to remove asbestos from school buildings in Morehead City, North Carolina. Other workers and I had to take a safety class before we could proceed. The instructor explained how we were to use our respirators, change the air filters, and perform other safeguards; and, luckily, there was no written test involved. Thereafter, I sewed mattresses for one company and even tried my hand at making fiberglass boats for another. On weekends, I found employment on a farm back in Stella, plowing fields and maintaining tractors by changing tires and pressure washing them. I also picked corn and baled hay. With every job, I worked hard and gave my all, but a lack of fulfillment dominated my thoughts. *There has to be more out there, but where do I find it with my limited education?* I wondered. Resultantly, a pattern was set, where I took on a variety of jobs in a quest to discover not only what occupation I was best at doing but the one that would leave me with a true sense of accomplishment and contentment within.

Always on the lookout for a more satisfying opportunity, I happened to be walking in Morehead City when I glanced from the sidewalk into a window of the local bus station. Something on the other side of the glass captured my attention, and I peered closer and noticed brochures for the U.S. Job Corps. I detoured inside, checked out the information, and took one of the attached business cards. As I studied it, I thought back to Career Day in high school and remembered a military recruiter speaking about the Job Corps. The next morning I called the number to set up a meeting.

The appointment was fruitful, and much to my family's

surprise, I was accepted into a program in Franklin, North Carolina, to train as a cook at the Lyndon B. Johnson Job Corps Center, operated by the United States Forest Service. I was on cloud nine! Franklin was almost a seven-hour drive from Stella, which meant I needed to move. Although the anticipation left me a little rattled, my joy outweighed it. Because I was leaving home and one of my younger brothers was getting a job and needed a vehicle, I gave him my Pontiac T-1000 and packed my belongings in preparation for the bus ride west. I was looking forward to being on my own and proving to myself I could be successful.

Upon arrival in Franklin, a green Job Corps van met and transported me to the base together with other trainees. It was around the month of May, and as I rode along inhaling the fresh air, I took in the scenery. Lush green hills and trees were everywhere. It was also the first time I had viewed mountains, and their beauty and vastness embedded in my memory. The twenty-minute ride seemed to zip by, and before I knew it, we had arrived at the base. We exited the van, were handed a list of rules and regulations, signed in, picked up our uniforms, and were taken to the barracks to get settled.

Once the curriculum began, other trainees and I alternated between one week of vocational training and one week of educational instruction. The majority of training was at the Job Corps center, but we would often be driven in a van to Southwestern Community College to cook in their gourmet chef's kitchen and learn more about the culinary arts. Additionally, we participated in various community cooking activities. During vocational training, the kitchen manager never let on he knew of my lack of academic ability, but I sensed he was aware. He would periodically leave me in charge if he had a meeting to attend, and he'd give me roll call schedules and menus in advance so I could learn them, which kept me ahead of the game.

In the educational realm of training, some instructors did work with me one-on-one, and I always had to stay two steps ahead. For example, if there was a test on Friday, most people would be able to study a day or two before in order to do well. I, on the other hand, would have to start studying a full week ahead. Many times I'd attempt to memorize the material as soon as I found out there was to be an exam or quiz. And when it was time to be tested, I'd hope for lots of true or false questions since they were easier for me.

Outside of studying, the Job Corps would give trainees who weren't restricted to quarters the option of traveling into Franklin, Silver, or sometimes Asheville by bus to shop or attend a movie on Fridays and Saturdays. When we embarked I always endeavored to obtain a window seat. Routinely, I would stare outside as if I were examining a fine painting. Our driver would proceed through hills and valleys that resembled being on a roller coaster, and I focused on the intricate architecture of houses, noticing some were built on cliffs in the mountains. As the seasons changed, I observed a spectrum of picturesque sights: gold, red, and orange leaves were projecting from trees in the fall, and the branches were sometimes covered with snow and glistening ice in the winter. As we'd roll into town, I always noticed the wide variety of stores and businesses, especially those in high-rise buildings since the architecture in my hometown had only been one-story.

Arriving at our destination, I'd jump to my feet, and the second the bus door opened, I'd whisk out like a genie in a bottle—unleashed! For me, browsing in large stores with endless options and various brand names was akin to being left to explore Disney World. As a youngster I didn't get to shop, other than at a convenience store. And throughout high school, I had only heard fellow students talk about attending movies at a theater, but I'd never been. In fact, the first film I saw in a cinema was with fellow trainees from the Job Corps. I was awestruck and thought the big screen and surround sound were the best things since sliced bread!

One month before graduation, the cafeteria manager said the center director for the Lyndon B. Johnson Job Corps and local U.S. Forest Service wanted to speak to me. I cringed, thinking the center director might want to kick me out of the Job Corps program due to my low educational level. However, when I went into his office, he revealed he'd heard good things from my instructors, and he complimented my cooking skills. He acknowledged that the staff and students looked up to me as a role model, and he liked the way I advised students to handle their personal problems without fighting. "You might have a bright future here with us when you graduate," he stated.

After I'd completed training and shortly before graduation, the center director called me into his office once again. This time he informed me, "I have to give all applicants a chance, but your name is on our list. Would you be interested in working for the U.S. Forest Service?" "Yes, I would!" I replied. As I walked out of his office, I reflected on what a great experience my training had been and how it had left me with a sense of direction. *I would love to come back here and work,* I concluded.

On December 20, 1988, I graduated from the Job Corps. Although no one was able to show up to support me, I was so proud of myself!

A couple of months later, the center director for the U.S. Forest Service and Job Corps in Franklin, North Carolina, contacted me again, this time by phone. "I'm calling to offer you a job as a cooking instructor for the United States Forest Service," he officially said. I was overjoyed and happily accepted the position as a staff member, teaching young adults, ages sixteen and up, how to cook. As I hung up the phone, I felt like a Marine; no more trenches for now. A huge sandbag had been lifted off of me. All my life I'd felt as if I were at war with myself and society, on American soil. I looked to the heavens and immediately voiced, "Wow—thank you for opening this door!"

On the job, I sometimes made schedules by following a previous schedule. I had to know every area of the kitchen and had to study the students' names in advance so I could give them their assigned areas in which to work. Some of my students would be cooking meats, vegetables, or pasta while others were preparing fruits, breads, desserts, beverages, or other menu items. There were three shifts, and I mostly worked the night shift or the breakfast shift. We served students and staff and averaged 150 or more people at each meal. Needless to say, my family members were astonished at my success.

Sometimes I was in charge of inventory, which wasn't easy, but once I developed a system, it wasn't as difficult as I'd thought. I had to prepare a couple of days before. The average person could probably do it during his or her shift, but I needed the head start. I'd stay after work and try to memorize where everything was in the dry and liquid storerooms and in the coolers and freezers. I'd copy names of items from cans, packages, bags, containers, and bottles. Thereafter, each time products were used, I'd cross them out on my list, making it easier and faster for me to complete inventory on Friday. When I had to check in stock, I'd ask my boss in advance if he had ordered anything different. He'd tell me, and I'd jot it down on paper as well as I could so I wouldn't be caught off guard when it was delivered.

One morning, I awoke from my cozy bed in the bachelor's quarters at 3:30 a.m. to be in the kitchen by 4:00. After putting on my uniform, I inserted a kitchen thermometer in the top pocket of my white jacket along with a pen and pencil and headed to the cafeteria. Upon arrival, I followed my usual routine: I turned on ovens, making sure they heated properly, followed by dishwashers, using my thermometer to be sure water temperatures reached 120 degrees. Next, I verified coolness in refrigerators and freezers and logged all readings down on a form attached to a clipboard hanging on the wall. I then filled a couple of sinks, measuring the water temperatures as well, so I could start some of the prep work for breakfast. The students came in at six. Typically, the cafeteria manager arrived at eight, but that particular day he needed to be away, so he had left me in charge.

Breakfast went off without a hitch, and my students and I made final preparations for the lunch crowd. As the students were serving lunch, I glanced toward the cafeteria entryway and saw a man carrying a briefcase. He neared me, and I could view his badge. As he introduced himself, he explained, "I'm here to do a routine health and safety inspection." I wasn't prepared for that, and I think my heart skipped a beat, but I couldn't do anything but proceed. I assigned one of the students to be in charge so I could walk around with the state food and health inspector. The inspector checked everything, from appliance temperatures to dates on packages in refrigerators and freezers. He made sure dry goods and liquids were kept in separate storerooms, and all had to be at least five inches from the floor. He even inspected corners of the dining hall, baseboards, and the bathrooms too. When we finished the tour, we sat at a table where he handed me a piece of paper. "Here you go. You passed inspection," he announced. "Wow, we passed!" I acknowledged.

When the cafeteria manager returned the next day, he was extremely happy. As the good news spread, the center director showed up unannounced at lunchtime one day along with a few of his colleagues. He walked right up to me and stated, "I heard about the inspection and wanted to personally shake your hand!" Then he added, "I also hear you make great food, especially scalloped potatoes, so we're here to try them!"

Although many students and staff thought I was a genius in my field, I eventually resigned from the U.S. Forest Service because I felt in my heart I was cheating the students. I believed it was wrong for trainees to be smarter than their instructor. Even though they didn't know my secret, the secret alone was beating me. To chance one student finding out was my greatest fear because they looked to me as a role model. They turned to me, not only for cooking instruction but also for advice about life, and I didn't want to disappoint them by blowing my cover. It wasn't only about me being hurt anymore, it was about the kids. Like an NBA player, I wanted to leave while I was still on top in the eyes of the kids.

Chapter Nine

While training with the Job Corps, I met a young lady, and we wed after I left the U.S. Forest Service. Because of the fears I had, I worked hard to keep my learning obstacles a secret from her. It was a daily struggle, but I succeeded. We started out in North Carolina where I found a job in an auto body shop prepping cars to be painted. A few years later, I heard of a construction job at a nearby military base and began as a bricklayer's helper, working my way up to become a bricklayer.

It was while we were in North Carolina that my wife gave birth to our lovely daughter. Our child was perfect, and I thought she was the most beautiful baby I'd ever seen. I was so proud of her. Whether she needed to be fed, changed, or bathed, I always jumped in to help. I was happy to simply spend time with her. She was a fun-loving little girl, and she grew to enjoy bath time in the kitchen sink. She'd hold a yellow rubber duck and slam it, without direction, into the water, splashing drops onto her face. Her reaction was comical as she squinted, smiled, and giggled. Off and on, I would flick a few drops of water on her face during bath time too, and she'd give the same good-humored response. Other times, I'd tell her she was an airplane as I raised her high into the air and made sound effects to mimic a plane's engine. We'd twirl around the living room as she laughed uncontrollably. Then I'd give her a big hug, and she'd usually rest her little head on the crook of my shoulder. She was the highlight of my day, and I couldn't wait to get home from work to see my little bundle of joy!

When she became a toddler I would talk to her, trying to give her my knowledge of the world, and a lot of our interactions took place outdoors. Both my daughter and I enjoyed being outside among nature; and, lucky for us, there was a vast wooded area near our home. Time and again, we'd roam through the woods, like Daniel Boone, looking at squirrels and birds. With every step, we could hear the rustle of leaves and the sound of tiny branches breaking beneath our feet. My daughter was so intrigued by everything she would stop and stare like a deer in the headlights. She'd often ask questions or make comments about the sights and sounds. When she spoke she would frequently run her words together, and her teeny voice was as cute as a button. As we strolled down wooded trails, she would ramble on, and it sounded as though I were hiking through the woods with a mini version of Daffy Duck.

Sometimes we'd just stand still feeling the wind on our faces as gusts would force their way through the branches of trees, sending their leaves into an acrobatic flutter, landing them at our feet. My little girl would smile brightly and raise her hands with her palms up toward the sky, as if it were snowing leaves.

Other times, we'd take a small plastic bowl and pick wild blueberries or blackberries. We'd walk back, hand in hand, until we made it into the front yard; then my daughter would break away and run full speed ahead to find her mother and announce, "We found berw-wees!"

One day, as my happy-go-lucky daughter and I hiked through the woods, we wandered down a trail we'd taken many times before. However, this time a large limb had broken and tumbled from a nearby tree, landing right across our pathway. I stepped over it and told her to do the same. She stopped in her tracks and looked at me in disbelief as she pointed to the limb. She shook her head from side to side. "Dad, no," she said in her high-pitched voice. "Yes, you can. You can do it," I responded. From her facial expression, you would have thought I'd asked her to step over a large oak tree. However, I could almost see the wheels turning in her little brain as she placed her tiny hands on the branch and swung one small leg at a time over it. When she made it across she jumped up and down, then clapped and squealed with delight, "I did it, I did it!"

At night, my daughter and I would sit on the wooden bench swing hanging from our front porch as we looked at the stars and I spoke to her about life. Her mother would often open the front door and say, "Are you guys coming in tonight?" I was determined to give my daughter worldly knowledge as well as a formal education. She would not follow my educational path. I was getting her ready for the White House!

My little girl was still a toddler when her mother and I noticed she wasn't breathing correctly, so we took her to a pediatrician. He assured us she'd outgrow the problem. A short time later we noticed a small red mark on her face, and the pediatrician said it was a birthmark. However, the red mark continued to grow, and our daughter's breathing became more labored. We sought answers from various physicians, but no one knew exactly what was wrong. One told us it could be cancer. He decided to run a battery of tests, hoping to discover what the growth on our child's face actually was. But before the test results came back, we had to rush our two-and-a-half-year-old to the ER because she was having so much trouble breathing. The ER doctor took a look at her and ran a few tests. As soon as he received the lab results, he quickly declared, "I've seen this before. We need to send her by Life Flight to a hospital in Greenville right away!"

Unfortunately, my wife and I were not allowed to fly in the helicopter with our little one; we had to find our own way. It took us a couple of days to make arrangements and round up gas money to make the trip. Since the small, old car we owned had a history of breaking down, we weren't sure it would make the two-hour drive into Greenville. Despite the trip seeming to take longer than it actually did, the car held up, and we made it safely.

When we arrived at the hospital, the doctors informed us our child did have a form of cancer. As we entered her room, we were extremely happy to see our daughter; it had been torturous not being there. However, she didn't look quite the same. Medical personnel had performed a tracheotomy on her so she could breathe, and she had a temporary feeding tube hanging from her side. Plus, she was hooked up to all types of monitors. The sight of all of the equipment frightened me, but I remained strong.

My daughter stayed in the hospital quite a while, and there were times our family car would sputter and stall right in our driveway, and my wife and I couldn't drive into Greenville. Frequently I would start out walking and then thumb a ride so I could check on our child. Her mother and I had an understanding: if I found a ride, I'd take it. Eventually, I bought a used cream-colored Cadillac El Dorado with an odometer reading of over 100,000 miles, but it was the best I could afford. We pushed the car to its limits, driving back and forth to the hospital as often as possible. One weekend, one of my daughter's doctors asked, "Have you heard of the Ronald McDonald House here in Greenville?" We hadn't, so he explained, "It's basically a hotel for families who have sick children in the hospital. It operates from donations, and it's right across the street." He then directed us to get the proper paperwork that would state we had a child in the hospital and lived out of town.

Because I had to work, I couldn't stay at the Ronald McDonald House on weekdays, but my wife sometimes did. However, when I was there on a weekend, that's where I would leave my belongings and where I'd shower. Many times I'd just fall asleep and spend the night in a chair in my daughter's room after telling her stories. Because of her tracheostomy she couldn't speak, but seeing the sparkle in her eyes and the smile spread up to her cheeks, I could tell she enjoyed listening to the fairy tales my mind created and the stories of life back home.

Some weekends I didn't have gas money to get to Greenville, which tormented me. At times, I felt like I was being baptized and held under the water while fighting the whole time to come up. The stress had to be double for my daughter's mother; I was used to some suffering, but she was not.

Several of my family members visited my daughter in

the hospital, and I could tell by the looks on their faces they were scared for me. A few weeks later when I was at my parents' house, I happily told family my daughter was coming home soon; the doctors and nurses had trained her mother and me to care for her condition. Mom responded, "Your dad and I think you should leave her in the hospital a little while longer." Others chimed in in agreement. I was so angry. At one point I asked myself, *What planet are these people from? Because I don't know them!* I thought they would have been more supportive. Much to my surprise, right before I left that day Dad stood up and voiced, "We will support your decision."

When my daughter was finally released from the hospital, I felt like I'd received the greatest gift of all. I was as happy as I had been on the day she was born because I realized I was getting a second chance with her.

In spite of her trach and only being able to eat pureed "baby food," she remained a happy, spirited girl who loved to laugh and play. I enjoyed feeding her at night, and her mother and I kept her routines as close to normal as possible. My daughter and I continued to sit on the porch swing in the evenings, and I'd regularly sing the ABCs to her or recite numbers. During the day, she loved to be outside, often drawing pictures in the dirt with a stick. Although she couldn't walk as far, we continued to stroll short distances into the woods. I'd talk about a variety of topics, including animals, bugs, and plants we saw along the way, and she would smile and nod her head. She and I had a bond that couldn't be broken.

One morning when my daughter was five years old, I got up to go to work and didn't hear her playing in her bedroom as I normally did. As I entered her room, I saw her lying face up, on the bed. I called her name, but she didn't move. When I reached for her, she was as cold as a block of ice. Frantically, I tried to revive her, giving her mouth-to-mouth resuscitation through her trach. I ended up on the floor, rocking my little girl back and forth in my arms, begging God to bring her back. My emotions prevailed, and I was overcome with grief. As my eyes pooled with water, I looked down at her, and my tears overflowed onto her face, as if a dam had broken.

I felt the warmth of anger build inside me, like a wildfire out of control, and then I grew fearless. I looked to the heavens and shouted, "Why couldn't you take me instead?!?!?!" Sadly, my little princess had passed away.

The death of my daughter was overwhelming and extremely hard for me to accept. But there probably aren't words to describe how devastated her mother felt. Not taking anything away from myself or other fathers, I realized the bond between a woman and the child she had coveted and nurtured within for nine months was different and beyond recognition.

In an attempt to handle my grief, I would go outside at night and gaze up at the clear sky as the stars twinkled above, just as my daughter and I had done together many times before. After locating the largest, brightest, most sparkly star, I'd envision it was my baby girl saying, "Look, Daddy, I'm a star after all!" Other times, I'd imagine her tiny voice stating, "I know you like to run, Daddy. I'll meet you at the finish line one day."

Chapter Ten

F ollowing the death of my daughter, I thought it would be best for her mother to have the support of her parents, so we moved closer to them in the state of Mississippi. Right away I started looking for employment and landed a job painting ships at Ingalls Shipbuilding. After working long enough to not only save money but also earn vacation time, my wife and I decided to take a summer trip to Pensacola, Florida. The beach was beautiful, and I was intrigued by the old historical buildings downtown. As it turned out, we eventually relocated to the area.

Finding employment in Pensacola did not come easily. After the move, I filled out and submitted over thirty applications, but no one called me for an interview. I followed up but was routinely told employers were still deciding. A couple of companies advised me to complete a second application because they couldn't read part of what I'd written. I knew my penmanship wasn't the greatest, and my nervousness from having to fill out most of the paperwork on the spot didn't help. From then on I worked to improve my handwriting. Then, all of a sudden, I received a couple of calls for job interviews.

To make ends meet, I became a full-time asphalt paver and grader by day, and by night I put in thirty hours a week at the dog track. At the track, I eventually worked my way up to the position of head lead-out. That meant I'd walk out with the dogs and give orders to the other lead-outs. As time passed, I found a better job in a nursing home as a floor tech. Not only did it pay more but it also came with benefits, and later I attained a position preparing food in the kitchen. In addition, I mowed grass on the side.

Once, after meeting with a client about her lawn and jotting down a few notes, I realized I'd forgotten one of her requests. It was then I decided to purchase a cassette recorder to keep in my truck. After conversing with a client and taking notes, I would immediately retreat to my vehicle to record the information onto a cassette tape before I forgot anything. Playing it back helped my memory and kept me on track. When I purchased new lawn equipment, I'd also record the model, series, and price in case I misplaced the manual or receipt; it was similar to having a second brain. Recordings and paperwork were kept in my makeshift office, which was actually a small workshop next to the house. Even when I wasn't working, I would sometimes withdraw there and record myself pronouncing and spelling words; hearing them again improved my skills. Like a scientist, I ended up with piles of cassette tapes, but the method worked, and to this day, I sometimes use a recorder.

After ten years together and careful consideration, my wife and I agreed to get a divorce. I eventually moved to the other side of town and took on an additional part-time job baking biscuits for Hardee's.

Since my mother had been so critical of my educational abilities growing up, I was divorced for six years before I told her, or any relatives, about the mutual breakup. When I spoke to them on the phone, they'd sometimes ask how my wife was, and I would answer, "As far as I know, she's fine." When I finally let the cat out of the bag, Mom was stunned and upset and wanted to know why I hadn't informed the family. I told her I wanted to get my life back together before I let them know so they wouldn't think the breakup was because of my learning problems.

Following the divorce, I had good jobs, a beautifully furnished apartment, two nice cars, and a $79 per month storage unit. Life seemed to be looking up.

On my way from work one Friday, I caught wind of two people discussing a great place in town to go dancing.

Intrigued, I made a mental note of the establishment's name. For about a week, I pondered the idea of going there, and then curiosity got the best of me. So the following Saturday night, I threw on a casual outfit, drove there, paid the entry fee, and walked through the grand wooden doors around 11:00 p.m. A popular song was blasting from huge speakers. I ordered a glass of water and stood in a corner, observing as people boogied their cares away on the wooden floor under the large mirrored disco ball hanging from the ceiling. Colored lights flashed on them, seeming to add to their excitement. The atmosphere and music made me want to join in, but doubt crept in my mind. *I haven't danced since I was a teenager*, I thought, *and now I'm in my forties! Plus, I've never danced in public—only in a cornfield.* I stayed long enough to make my observations that night, then strolled to my car to head back to my apartment.

The ensuing week, I made up my mind to go back to the dance spot on the weekend. To prepare, I purchased new black dress slacks, a white button-down shirt, a black vest, and a white hat trimmed at the base with a black band. Previously, I had found a pair of saddle oxford shoes at a thrift store, so I taped them off to spiff them up by first using white shoe polish, then black. They matched my outfit perfectly—the best six dollars I'd ever spent!

When Saturday night arrived, I donned my clothes and felt as if I were coming to life. I headed out of my

LIKEWISE & VELVET SKIES

apartment to my car, arriving at my destination around 11:00 p.m. I paid the entry fee and entered the brick building through the high arched doorway. As I crossed the threshold, I could already hear the tunes roaring, and the place was packed with patrons. I ordered a glass of water, as I'd done the week before, and watched as people invaded the dance floor. All of a sudden, my foot started twitching, and then moving up and down as it kept time with the music. I felt like an old Corvette that had been sitting: once I got cranked up and my engine revved, there was no stopping me. In short order, my glass of water was on a table and I was on the dance floor, bobbing, weaving, spinning, and gliding from one end to the other. Dancing had been on lockdown for so long, but it was all unleashed that night. I continued for hours and sweated so much my clothes looked freshly washed. Near closing time I left. Although I've never had therapy, the experience left me feeling as though I'd had a workout and therapy rolled into one. For years, I would frequent that locale on weekends just to enjoy dancing.

Subsequently, I was driving to the local military base one afternoon after work to meet friends. But my plans quickly came to a halt when I was involved in a car accident, which caused me to lose the only car I owned at that time. Because the mishap was my fault, it led to new expenses, and I found I could no longer afford my apartment.

Not sure where to go, the circumstances sent my mind scrambling, and I found myself at the local Waterfront Rescue Mission, looking for a place to stay. Over the years, I had run into people down on their luck and had sent them there, and I'd personally driven two people to this location for assistance, so I knew it was a good place. However, I never expected I'd be asking for the organization's help. As I entered the door of the downtown building, a priest shook my hand and offered me a seat so we could talk. I explained my situation, and he listened intently. Then he leaned forward and commented, "You look too healthy, and you're not an addict. Sorry, you can't stay here." He then directed me to check with another shelter on the other side of town. Not having money for a taxi, I made my way there by foot, which took a couple of hours. But my visit was short-lived as the director of that facility shook his head no. "You don't have a major medical issue, and you're not a substance abuser," he stated.

As I exited the warmth of the shelter, the sun was beginning to set and the temperature was steadily dropping. I wasn't sure what to do, but I knew time was of the essence. I walked along, eyes gazing downward at the sidewalk below, weighing my options, until something in my peripheral vision caused me to glance up. Next to a dumpster, lying on a cold concrete slab was a middle-aged man covered in a blanket, shivering. He appeared to be homeless, and I wondered what circumstances had forced him onto the streets. *Could he have fallen on hard times as I have?* As my shoes hit the concrete below, I sensed increased humidity in the air. Soon the sky grew darker as gray clouds rolled in and lingered overhead, and the north wind began to howl. *Where can I find shelter and safety?* I contemplated. Then, as suddenly as a streak of lightning, an idea flashed into my mind. *I won't find rent cheaper than that of my storage unit. Plus, I need to save as much money as possible to get back on my feet.* So my decision was made. I moved into my self-storage unit, along with my belongings, and ended up living there for about a year.

At the time, I was working a construction job and didn't have to be there until 8:00 a.m., but in an attempt to keep anyone from knowing where I was residing, I'd always leave before the sun came up to start the one-hour walk to work. I didn't have an alarm clock, but luckily, there was an old electrical outlet on a pole in close proximity to the unit that I was able to use to plug a timer into my floor lamp. The lamp was placed right next to my mattress and was set to turn on around 4:00 a.m. As soon as the light beamed in my face, I'd pop my head up, like bread in a toaster, quickly open the garage style door, and unplug the lamp so there would be no evidence of my dwelling inside.

If I finished work early, I'd often walk around town thinking, killing time until I could make the trek back to the storage unit, arriving after dark. After work, I'd fill a five-gallon bucket with water from a nearby spigot, using a tin can because the faucet was so low to the ground. I'd then carry the bucket inside, telling myself, *This is how they bathed in the old days: a pail of water and a piece of soap.*

Sometimes the water would be bitter cold. In that event, I'd plan ahead by filling the five-gallon container before work and setting it in the sun, hoping it would warm at least a little before nightfall.

I mostly ate canned goods because they didn't spoil, and the old electrical outlet came in handy; I just had to use it after dark. I'd often plug in my coffee maker and use its glass pot to warm up some of the canned goods or to heat water to make noodles or rice.

My storage unit was not climate controlled, and during the blazing summer it was comparable to a sauna. It was so hot and humid inside at times that I would be drenched with sweat; my eyes would sting, and I could taste the salt. Therefore, when I wasn't working, I would usually visit people, go into stores, or walk around until the sun went down. By then the temperature was cooler, and I could crack the door open to the storage unit and plug in a fan.

During the winter, it was very cold, but I would put on layers of clothes and socks, plug in a portable heater, and bundle up in my blanket. I'd often be awakened by the sound of my teeth chattering, yet I was thankful for the mild winters in Pensacola, as compared to my hometown of Stella.

Many times, I would hear noises in the ceiling and assume they were from squirrels coming in for the evening, like I had. Sometimes the repetitive running and scratching was so intense one would have thought they were up there break dancing. Therefore, I'd leave a fan plugged in to try to muffle the sounds.

One night, as I lay in darkness on my mattress, I dozed off but was awakened by something falling on my face. I quickly slapped myself, thinking it could have been a spider, but desperately hoping it wasn't. I fumbled for a nearby flashlight and was relieved to discover only a tiny piece of insulation had fallen from the ceiling above. As I shined the light upward, I noticed part of the plastic ceiling was torn. Then, in an instant, like jacks-in-the-box, out popped the furry heads of two of the largest wood rats I'd ever seen! Their eyes reflected the light and looked red as they seemed to glare at me, hovering above. The rats were so big they put me in mind of the movie *Jurassic Park*, and I felt as if someone had just poured cold water all over me. Boy, did I cringe! That night I didn't get much sleep, but as the morning unfolded, I slid the door up, and sunlight came rushing in, causing the rats to disappear. That was my opportunity to climb on top of my belongings with a roll of duct tape to repair the hole.

Eventually, the wood rats chewed through the duct

tape, and I repeatedly patched the holes. As time progressed, I'd often see the long-tailed creatures outside my storage unit at night. I think they smelled the food I had, so I purchased a thick plastic bin with a lid and placed my dry goods inside. In spite of my actions, the battle with the rats continued, but I must have had an angel in the midst, because I remained safe.

To keep my mind from focusing on my less-than-desirable circumstances, I continued to hit the dance floor on weekends. In fact, it wasn't until I took up residency in the storage unit that I realized how important dancing was to me. It gave me something to look forward to and ended up saving me in the process.

On a typical Friday or Saturday night, I'd open a package of ramen noodles, break up its contents into my coffee pot, add water, and plug in the coffee maker. Once the noodles were heated, I'd pour them into a bowl, and that was dinner. Next, I'd bathe and brush my teeth using water from the outside spigot. I would put on deodorant, cologne, and my best clothes, then walk about thirty minutes to the well-known business with its beckoning dance floor. After living in the storage unit for two months, I saved enough money to purchase a bicycle, which really cut down my travel time. I continued to dress my best and pedal to the establishment Friday and Saturday nights, arriving at 11:00 p.m., dancing on a speaker, and cutting a rug on the main floor until 2:00 a.m. While I was getting down on the dance floor, life couldn't get any better, and that was as high as I got. When it was time to leave, I always exited the building alone; I wasn't looking for anything other than to take joy in moving to the music. Dancing kept me from thinking of life's negatives and was a fun way to escape reality. It made me feel like I was in another world.

While living in the storage unit, a friend told me Special Olympics needed volunteers, so I decided I would help. I had a soft place in my heart for children, especially after losing my own child. Plus, I thought the idea of continuing to volunteer would be a good way to make my abnormal living situation seem more normal. Upbeat, I climbed on my bicycle and pedaled to a local sports association, seeking information about Special Olympics. I was planning to pick up the necessary forms, take them with me, fill them out, and return them the next day. But to my surprise, the lady behind the counter asked, "Could you fill out the volunteer forms here? It will keep you from having to come back." As I glanced around the room, all eyes were on me, and I felt pressured to oblige. She handed me a clipboard containing papers, and as I looked at the requested information and abbreviations written in tiny print, some letters and numbers seemed to move and trade places on the form. I felt my temperature rise and found myself growing anxious. I realized the Ghost of Inability to Learn had followed me into the building. I placed the clipboard back on the counter and eased it toward the lady. "I left my ID in the car," I told her. I exited the building and headed for my bike in the parking lot.

I would have done just about anything the Special Olympics association asked, whether it was to pass out water or to help set up equipment. I was very disappointed in myself. I wished I hadn't been too scared to tell the lady I wasn't really good with reading and writing, but my parents' voices played in my mind like an old record, reminding me to keep my secret. I knew some people in society were not forgiving and could be extremely judgmental, and I didn't want to chance the humiliation.

Eventually, I made it out of the storage unit, got a new apartment, and found myself at letter A fighting my way to Z again. Negative things had such an impact on my life; they were hard to forget, but I had to in order to move forward. Not judging anyone and meaning no disrespect, in spite of challenges, I never pacified myself by smoking, drinking, or doing drugs. Those things could have put me on a faster road to death, and I chose: not.

Chapter Eleven

Subsequently, I changed jobs and began working as a cook in a nursing home again. When I wasn't in the kitchen, I'd talk to the men and women residing in the facility, and I'd often volunteer there on my days off. Sometimes I cooked a few meals at my apartment to deliver to certain occupants whose family members hadn't shown up to visit them for a while; I think it made them feel special. I know they thought I was there to help them, but in actuality, after listening to their stories, which sometimes made me laugh and other times made me cry, I realized they were helping me focus on and be appreciative of the positive aspects of my life. There was so much to be learned from the residents and their experiences.

I also enjoyed entertaining the nursing home's

residents. On more than one occasion, I dressed up as the Easter Bunny and passed out eggs and candy as I hopped and kicked up my heels around the main dining room. Employees would bring their kids, and the residents and I had a great time interacting with the children. Then I'd make my way to the rooms of those individuals who couldn't participate in the festivities. In spite of the rising temperature in the bunny suit as I jumped like a real rabbit on a trampoline, the roars of laughter and smiles on the people's faces made it all worthwhile. Other times, I'd sing or dance for them in the main hall or serenade them in their rooms. I was once asked by a family to sing at a resident's funeral, and I was very honored to do so. Getting to know nursing home residents has been one of the high points of my life.

There were times I ventured to other nursing homes to entertain and visit the residents. Several facilities were owned by the same person who owned the one where I worked, and as long as I had that inside connection, I didn't have to fill out any paperwork permitting my entry. However, on one occasion when visiting a different facility, I was presented with a couple of forms and asked to promptly fill them out. I noticed beads of sweat pop out on my forehead, then trickle down my face, and it felt as if my insides were dancing the jitterbug. Although I was dressed up, ready to perform, the facility's requirements made me so tense I walked out. Most of my life, when anyone would bring me paperwork to read and sign or someone asked me to write down something, I would feel an overwhelming sense of pressure and awkwardness. Sometimes, it wasn't that I couldn't do it, but the Ghost of Inability to Learn had followed me so long it had left its impact.

When I wasn't working, I'd often train and run in races; sometimes, for fun; other times, to support a cause such as breast cancer. Once I was practicing for the Pensacola Double Bridge Run when a spider fell out of a tree onto my arm. I shook the spider off and didn't realize it had bitten me. That Saturday morning, I woke up to go to the race, like I'd done years before, and I was fine. However, after completing the fifteen-kilometer run, I went out dancing that night for three hours and then returned home. I woke up the next day, feverish and dizzy, to the sound of my doorknob being jimmied. I shuffled my way to the door, turned the knob, and peered through the small opening. There stood a pastor with a church flier in his hand. He jumped back and commented, "You look sweaty. You must have had a good time last night." I replied, "No. I think I was bitten by a spider." Then I showed him my swollen wrist and hand. He told me I'd been bitten by a brown recluse and stressed, "You need to go to the ER right away because they eat the flesh from the inside out!"

I took the pastor's advice, checked in at the front desk of the emergency room, had a seat, and waited my turn to be seen. Sitting amongst others, I observed a large clock mounted to the wall, and as the minute hand made a full rotation and the hour hand eased to the following hour, I concluded I was going to be there a while. I was supposed to have dinner with a friend and his family that evening, but as time ticked on, it didn't look like I would be out of the ER in time, so I gathered quarters from my pockets and made my way to the pay phone in the waiting area. I dialed, the phone rang, and my friend's wife answered. I let her know I thought I'd been bitten by a brown recluse, was in the ER, and couldn't make it to dinner. She understood and wished me well. I hung up the phone and sat back down to continue waiting.

In short order, three doctors approached me. They first confirmed my name and then escorted me to one of the rooms. *Is a spider bite that serious? Am I dying?* I wondered. Much to my surprise, my friend, who happened to be a physician, had called a few colleagues to help me. One doctor even handed me his cell phone and told me my friend was going to call me on it. The ER staff got right to work. My temperature was 103 degrees and climbing, and by that time my right wrist, arm, and thigh were extremely swollen. Doctors agreed: I had been bitten by a brown recluse, and the poison was spreading throughout my body. Immediately, they administered an IV and made small cuts on my wrists and thighs where they inserted tubes to drain fluids.

The following morning, my friend, his wife, and their two sons and daughter were at my bedside checking on me. I was very surprised to see them because I knew they were driving out of town for a family vacation that day. When I questioned them about it, my friend's wife spoke up, "We were headed out of town but decided to postpone our vacation. We can't leave you in the hospital without anyone to check on you!"

As it turned out, I ended up staying with my friend and his family for three months while I recovered. Their young daughter was amused at the way I would "duck walk" up and down the stairs due to my medical procedure, and her parents genuinely cared about me. They were one of the greatest families I had ever met!

In fact, my physician friend and his wife were the only couple who knew about my difficulties with learning aside from my family and teachers. Neither my friend nor his wife believed I could have such a problem, but I did. They always told me I was smart in my own way. I once asked my friend, when he and I were driving to see a movie, if he could give me a new brain since he was a doctor in a hospital. He gave me a curious look, as if he'd been startled, and responded, "If I do that, you may not know us anymore. Don't be ashamed of who you are and what you know. There are others in the world who would love to have your abilities. It's not your fault; you're just wired that way." Then he grinned, and I did too.

Eventually, like a vampire in a film, I rose from the dead and made the move back to my apartment.

Chapter Twelve

I n time, I looked for ways other than my own to enhance my education, which led me to a local college to inquire about general educational development classes. I was told to return on a Tuesday evening to be tested, so I did. Standing outside the designated testing room, I reached for the doorknob, and my heart rate increased. It was like I was in the movie *Jaws*—I was on edge. When I stepped inside there were nineteen others in attendance, so I took a seat in the back. A lady passed out test booklets, answer sheets, paper, and pencils and announced the exam was timed. I could feel nerves tingle in my hands, and the sensation worked its way up my arms until the tension caused a slight headache. I became warm as wet beads of perspiration trickled from my forehead to my ears. I shook my hands to loosen them in preparation for the task at hand, and then the test began.

One by one, the other nineteen test takers, who happened to be much younger than I was, finished early and handed in their work. I felt as nervous as a cat on a hot tin roof. Twice I planned to walk out of the room before completion, but I told myself I'd never get anywhere if I quit, so I remained until I was no longer allowed and time was up. Proud of my determination, yet uneasy about my score, I turned in my exam, bade the test administrator a good evening, and made my exit.

I had parked a distance away, and as I proceeded toward my car, I felt my vital signs return to normal. I breathed a sigh of relief, happy the night's stressful situation was behind me. Reaching my vehicle, I sat inside and said aloud, "This can't keep happening." I mulled over the incident, as well as others I'd had of a similar nature. Over the years, I learned to give things names to help me deal with them, so I came up with my own term for what I had experienced—"spiking anxiety." To combat it, I realized I had to act like an FBI investigator and first assess a situation, then map out what I needed to do to best manage it. I was determined not to keep letting "spiking anxiety" get the best of me.

The following week, I drove to the college to start GED classes. The teacher motioned me to her desk to discuss my test scores, as she did with all enrollees.

Unfortunately, I hadn't done as well as I'd hoped, but she assured me everyone in the classroom was on a different level and we'd all be striving to improve. I let her know up front that I'd probably be her lowest-level student and requested to work alone, as opposed to participating in classroom or group activities. She agreed, and I sought a seat. But because I was the last to enter the room, I had to take the only available chair at a table beside another student. I had nothing against the student; it was my uneasiness that created an issue because I didn't want anyone to view the remedial level of material I was studying. Hence, I resolved to be the first in the classroom in the days to follow so I could pick a prime seat. I always chose the front table, near the far wall, furthest from the main door. That way, when other students entered and exited, they didn't pass by me and couldn't glance at my work. I'd also place my backpack in the empty chair beside me and spread a few papers or a notebook out so the area would look more occupied, hopefully edging classmates to sit elsewhere. Most of the time my routine worked, but when it didn't, I'd try to cover some of my classwork with a notebook or blank piece of paper. I couldn't control everything in the room, but managing what I could kept my "spiking anxiety" at bay.

When I entered the classroom, I would ordinarily get a workbook and complete exercises at my own pace—everything from English grammar to spelling, reading comprehension, history, science, and math. When finished, I would have the instructor check my answers. Other times, I'd have questions about words or math problems and make my way to the teacher's desk, hoping she didn't answer too loudly and cause unwanted attention to be focused on me. Sometimes she would look my way and say, "If you want to participate in this class activity, you can; but if not, you can work in your workbook." Most of the time I kept my nose in my workbook.

In the midst of each four-hour class, we were given a twenty-minute break. Most looked forward to it, but I didn't. My instinct was to avoid chatting with my classmates because invariably they would ask, "What level are you on?" or "When are you taking your GED test?" If I saw acquaintances who were taking college level classes, I tried to avoid them. These situations would send me reeling back to my school days as an adolescent. From time to time, I'd encounter a friend in the hall, and he or she would ask what I was studying. Not wanting to lie, I'd simply reply, "General classes—English, math." Outside the educational realm, I felt I could conquer the world; and for some reason, my self-esteem was way above average. But in the classroom, my confidence plummeted, like the temperature during an Alaskan winter.

In spite of a few uncomfortable situations, the longer I stayed in GED, the more accustomed to it I became, and the benefits far outweighed the drawbacks. I discovered the classes helped a lot, especially after I was able to relax and get into a routine. Once, I told my teacher, "I'll be one hundred before I get my GED!" She gave a simpering smile and replied, "At least you're trying. Just keep trying." I thought, *If she only knew how hard I've been trying...* Determined to make progress, I put my best foot forward, and by the end of the first year, I had surprisingly jumped a grade level in all subjects. Therefore, I continued to enroll in the classes. I felt I was making positive strides toward my education and my future.

Even in GED, I noticed words and letters were still flipping around like a big king mackerel on the end of a fishing line. So I set up an appointment to have my eyes checked. Because it was scheduled during class time, I told my teacher I'd be absent. She understood and wished me luck.

The result of the eye exam left me with the knowledge that I was nearsighted in my right eye. I spent nearly $500 on glasses, thinking they would not only improve my sight but also slow down some of the acrobatic letters I saw when reading. But to my disappointment, glasses didn't stop the words from moving like a gymnast, and I eventually found out the visual problems I'd endured were not with my eyes.

Once, in an attempt to seek answers, I went to a hotel where there was an Alcoholics Anonymous meeting, signed in, and sat in the back just to listen. I felt a little out of place since I had never tried alcohol, but I had heard wonderful things about AA. People told stories of alcohol and drug abuse as well as physical abuse. There were many sad stories; one woman had accidentally killed her baby by placing too many blankets on it while under the influence. The members clapped for each other, hugged, and seemed to have compassion for one another. I so wished I could tell them my story and feel some of the same support, but I knew they wouldn't really care unless I shared their afflictions, which I didn't. That night, I went home and prayed for the people at the meeting. My heart went out to them, especially the woman who had lost her child. In spite of the troubling stories, the experience was good for me.

Based on my limited encounters over the years, I concluded that most people didn't really care to help unless I had an addiction. Taking nothing away from those who are addicted, I do feel as if my inabilities are cousins to addiction. Just as alcohol or drug abuse can cause one to have difficulty getting hired, so can an inability. Similarly, substance abuse and an impairment like mine are not always visible to the naked eye. Nonetheless, living with either of them can cause one to fear being put under the microscope and found out. Then, there is always the chance of being ridiculed, turned down for promotions, or even terminated from a job; I had a lot of those same fears. Additionally, people with comparable conditions may question their own abilities, which could lead to them leaving an occupation or career prematurely.

I have discovered life's circumstances are similar to cancer in that they don't discriminate. Many nights, I prayed that no other child would have to experience the learning difficulties I had to endure. It's one thing to deal with society, but another to fight from within.

Chapter Thirteen

Over the years, I realized not only was the Ghost of Inability to Learn haunting me, but my childhood memories were nagging as well. Any time I had to go out of town, I would experience an internal frenzy because I was afraid I wouldn't be home when a bill arrived. Having seen my father miss electric and gas payments, made me realize the same could happen to me. Although I had the money to take care of the bills, I was worried about making payments on time, so as soon as a bill arrived, I'd mail in my check or take cash to the company personally.

In spite of my diligence, I arrived home one day to discover the power company had cut off my electricity, which sent me into an immediate panic. I knew I had paid my bill by cashier's check, so I jumped in my car and zipped to the power company, taking my copy of the check as proof. My insides were in turmoil. As I was standing in line, a security guard asked, "Young man, are you okay?" I told him I was, but as soon as I left the building, I recognized I wasn't. My fears were creating a noticeable condition. My cashier's check was eventually located; the company apologized and reconnected the power without charge.

My insecurities carried over into other areas, as well. When I took my first road trip out of town, I was a tense bundle of nerves. I had a gray Ford Crown Victoria at the time, and I took all precautions before traveling: I put air in the tires, got an oil change, and had the car checked from top to bottom. Yet, as I made the twelve-hour drive from North Carolina to Mississippi, every little weird sound the car made caused me to tense up more, and I didn't want to stop even for restroom breaks, for fear the ignition wouldn't start again once I turned it off. The whole trip was shadowed with thoughts of how unreliable my father's automobiles had been, as well as my own incidents where vehicles had left me in limbo. Although my Crown Vic successfully made the drive into Mississippi without incident, I practically had to pry my fingers from the steering wheel.

At one point, while working several jobs, I tried to accumulate four vehicles. I had three cars and was thinking about getting a motorcycle, just to increase my options in case one vehicle wouldn't run. When I had a car in the shop, I didn't want to accept a ride from a friend or anyone at the dealership; I preferred to walk home, regardless of the weather or distance. Seeing how my parents sometimes couldn't depend on others to help with transportation was deeply ingrained in my mind, as was the resulting disappointment on their faces. In turn, I didn't want to chance the same, so for a while I attempted to only depend on myself when it came to getting from one point to another. I later discovered my behavior wasn't something I had created out of the blue; rather, my mind was making transportation a larger issue due to what I had seen growing up.

One morning, shortly after I had first enrolled in GED, I got into my car to head to the college, only to find the ignition wouldn't start. Initially, I began to panic, then found myself on my bicycle making the fifteen-minute ride to the campus. I arrived safely, dabbed the perspiration from my head, straightened my dress clothes, and headed to class. Afterwards, my teacher saw me get on my bike and asked about my car. I just replied, "Riding my bike is good exercise." She smiled and I pedaled on. As I picked up speed, the wind began to gust and the sky grew dark, as though it were going to rain cats and dogs. However, I made it home before the bottom dropped out. I said out loud, "Not having a car isn't as terrible as I thought." That was a pivotal moment for me. I realized a couple of things:

1. My father went through a lot, yet still stood tall; I could be just as strong as he was, if not stronger.

2. Most importantly, it wasn't what happened, but how I reacted that affected me.

Thanks to that lightbulb moment, I was able to conquer my fears involving bills and transportation. In fact, as a form of therapy, I purposely didn't pay my electric bill one month; and, of course, my power was disconnected. I used a flashlight to move around my apartment at night, and after two days, I calmly went to the power company and paid the bill as well as the reconnection fee. I was able to maintain control of myself, and I realized it wasn't the end of the world to be without electricity or to have a bill lapse. The outcome depended on my reaction.

Chapter Fourteen

I t wasn't until a few years ago, when I had high school transcripts sent to a local college, that I found out what the educational system in North Carolina had written about me. The college counselor called me into her office. "You won't like what's on your transcript," she revealed.

I asked her to read it, and she hesitated at first. As she progressed, I was horrified to hear what had been officially noted about my ability to learn. The counselor could see I was visibly shaken and asked if I wanted to remain in her office to calm down, but I declined. She handed me a copy of the transcript, and I thanked her and left.

Exiting her office, I reflected on the words she had read, and my mind went back to school days. I wondered if that was how people had seen me. I also thought about how the carpentry teacher had treated me and realized he must have known what was on the paper. I became overwhelmed with emotions and had to dart into a restroom to throw up. The Ghost of Inability to Learn was back, still haunting me, but this time was worse. It's one thing to be told you're stupid your whole life, but another to see what had been documented and kept on file. As long as I live, I'll never forget the counselor reading that to me. I have to admit I was distraught for quite a while, and I dare not disclose the transcript's contents.

Afterwards, I didn't know if I should call my mother and tell her about the transcript, because if she had already known about it, I don't think I could have forgiven her for how I was treated. However, I decided to be brave and tell my mother what was written on the transcript, since Dad had previously passed away. She was obliterated by what I said and started crying.

I asked if she'd ever received papers with the same or similar information before. "No! Your father and I never heard it from a teacher or saw it on a document from the school," she said, her voice trembling. She apologized profusely for the way she and my father had treated me as I was growing up and asked me for a copy of the transcript. However, I had been so ashamed and upset that I had burned my copy.

I started doing my own research, and my physician

friend and his wife helped by purchasing books and calling experts in the field of learning. I was overwhelmed with the information we found and decided to set up an appointment with an out-of-town doctor who was a specialist in the areas of cognition and comprehension. I boarded a plane and was looking forward to getting answers. I was very optimistic.

When the doctor first called me back to have a seat in his office, he told me he had a hunch as to my diagnosis, just based on the paperwork I had to fill out at the front desk, but he performed a number of written and verbal tests before he concluded why learning had always been so challenging for me. "You have a learning disability called dyslexia and an additional disability," he said. "You are dyslexic with numbers and letters, randomly seeing them move forward and backward, and it's worse with words and sentences since letters are so close together and can appear to trade places. Copying information and sounding out words may also pose problems." He went on to explain, "Furthermore, unless you really focus on reading, you may lose concentration. You can do it, but you have to focus more intently than most, and the dyslexia doesn't help." He followed up with, "It's no wonder reading and writing can be difficult for you." He told me I could work to improve, but pointed out, "There is no cure for dyslexia."

As I left from my appointment that day, I had a lump in my throat, and I fought back tears. I realized the Ghost of Inability to Learn had joined forces with dyslexia. It had super-sized itself. I couldn't believe I'd flown so far away to get disappointing news. Nevertheless, I was determined not to let my learning disabilities win; I vowed to keep fighting until the day I die.

Not wanting to accept the newly found diagnosis that came without a cure, I decided to go back to an eye doctor, hoping technological advances might help me get a diagnosis stating the problems were with my eyes, not my brain, and lead me to some sort of cure in the form of glasses or contact lenses. However, my hopes slowly deflated, like a balloon containing a pinhole, as the ophthalmologist revealed nothing more than the fact that I'd become a little more nearsighted in one eye. I left with a bill and a prescription for new glasses. Once again, as magic gone wrong, glasses didn't do the trick.

A month later, I received a phone call from the doctor's office where I had been diagnosed with dyslexia and an additional learning disability, requesting I come in for a follow-up appointment. I complied and was surprised to discover the doctor had ordered and received copies of my elementary and high school transcripts. He began, "The people who wrote those comments on your transcripts would be absolutely shocked to meet you today." He shook his head as if he was baffled, and elaborated, "Considering your diagnosis, I'm extremely surprised you don't have a speech problem. From where I stand, you sound very intelligent, and it seems you try hard. Just by talking to you, the average person would never know."

Chapter Fifteen

I've been wired this way since birth, so I am not trying to blame teachers, the school system, or my parents. Who is to blame? No one. The schools didn't have the means and technology now available; otherwise, they might have been able to better detect my disabilities at an early age, and maybe someone would have known how to effectively teach a kid like me. My parents thought I wasn't trying hard enough, and individuals within the school system reinforced that belief by stating the same. I believe Mom and Dad did the best they could with the resources and knowledge they had at the time; I can't fault them for what they didn't know. They were aware of the importance of a solid education, and because I didn't perform well in that area, they pushed me. In my heart, I know they loved me and didn't intend any harm. To the contrary, they thought they were helping.

While staring outside one cool fall morning, I noticed the oaks and pines tremble as the wind wisped between them like a ballet dancer, causing pine cones to tumble to the earth below, and I couldn't help but be drawn back to my childhood. Like a bear climbing a tree, I, too, was left with some scars. Although I've moved forward, I realized so many punishments, including whippings, could have been eliminated if my parents had only had a clear understanding of what was wrong with me.

On a positive note, the fact that I didn't know why I couldn't read or write well kept me striving for success. Like a rooster running after feed, I was determined. Over the years, by trying to read books and working with numbers on my own as well as in classes, my education has improved. I have attended literacy programs, GED classes, and often stayed after class, a few days a week, for tutoring. On several occasions, I sat in on university classes, taking a seat in back to observe. I was amazed by the professors' articulation and teaching methods and was fascinated by the way students seemed to pull information out of the air and document it so quickly. My mind was moving one hundred times a minute; and, yes, I was lost, yet I wasn't. I felt like a kid in a candy store and always left with newfound knowledge. I have never stopped trying to learn, and I will never give up on learning. The world is my Webster's dictionary. If events are positive, I use them, not only for myself but to help others. If incidents are negative, I can often extract a positive from them.

Looking back, I was able to gain a lot of wisdom from being bullied. Bullies enjoy picking on people who are different, and due to my poor performance in school, dressing in hand-me-down clothes, and being poor, I became a victim. When I was young, I should have told a teacher or other adult that I was being badgered, but I didn't. Not only would it have helped me but I might have stopped young bullies from becoming even bigger bullies as adults. I could possibly have saved them from a future of fights, jail time, or even death resulting from harassing the wrong person.

However, as I got older I discovered tactics to keep bullies at bay. I eventually realized they wanted a reaction from me; they'd look at my eyes, body language, and facial expressions to see what kind of response I would give. At the first sign of me being uncomfortable, they knew they'd found a weakness, and they focused on that insecurity repeatedly. Unfortunately, I even had a teacher do that to me, and I would recommend that anyone in a similar situation report the incident to a higher authority.

The following are my suggestions for kids, teenagers, and adults on how to deal with bullies:

1. When bullies make comments to you, just smile.

2. Repeat back to them what they say (minus profanity) so they can hear how stupid they sound.

3. Ask, "Is that your opinion of me or of yourself?" Frequently, bullies are insecure about themselves or their families or they're jealous, causing them to target another's weakness to feel better about themselves.

4. Calmly walk away. Sometimes the best reaction is no reaction at all.

In the world in which we live, bullying is alive and well among people of all ages; it often goes by the names "pressure," or "peer pressure." It exists everywhere—in schools, at work, at social events, and, believe it or not, it's even in some religious institutions. These days, bullying travels at warp speed in the forms of cyber- and text bullying. Although I wish I had never been bullied, those experiences helped form me into the person I am today. I was able to gain knowledge, insight, and strength, and I have been able to help my family and friends with advice as a result.

Over the course of my life, I have also encountered and observed something I have come to term "**nice-nasty.**" It's when someone gives a compliment, which is nice, immediately followed by criticism, which is nasty. I only consider it bullying if it's done to the same person repeatedly, as my carpentry teacher did to me in high school. Typically, a "nice-nasty" is not bullying and is said on a whim. Most people don't even see it coming because they are focused on the positive comment and aren't armed for the negative one. For example: Woman A tells woman B, "Your hair looks great today!" While woman B smiles from ear to ear and responds, "Thank you," woman A follows up with, "But you could have left those shoes in the store." Woman B is now stunned by the nasty comment. Why give a compliment if you're going to snatch the rug out from under the person within an instant?

People in society may tell you there is something wrong with you, causing you to carry a lunch box of tools, repeatedly trying to fix yourself. However, the problem may not be with you; it could possibly be them. If you realize the issue isn't with you and you do not speak up, treat them as the kings or queens they are and give them your self-esteem on a platter. Standing up for yourself the first time may feel awkward. Keep in mind: you are only trying to make a wrong right by defending yourself. Much like a musician, the more you practice, the better you will become. As a result, you will gain confidence and others won't mistake your kindness for weakness.

One of the biggest hurdles I had to overcome was fear. My personal interpretation is that there are two kinds.

Fear 1 (external): is visible and mostly created by others; it can be seen when one receives a devastating diagnosis, news of a loved one being in an accident or dying, or even when one is intentionally scared by another.

Fear 2 (internal): is created within and remains there

unless one decides to reveal it; it can arise if a vehicle is being repossessed, a divorce takes place, or in situations where there is a fear of failure.

Most of my fears were internal because they were created within myself, and I chose for them to remain there as I fought from within. However, I've developed ways to manage. People need to realize no one is perfect, even if he or she seems to be. Accept the fact that although some things can be made better, they cannot always be changed. Most of all, don't allow fear to make a home in you.

For a time, I knew I had allowed fear to become my roommate, so I decided to take matters into my own hands. One day, as I was heading out my front door, I looked back and shouted, " Fear, I'm evicting you from this mind and body, and don't you ever come back again!" Right before I exited, I looked back over my shoulder and yelled, "Doubt, that goes for you too! You're also evicted!" Then I forcefully shut the door leaving Fear and Doubt behind.

"**Spiking anxiety**" is different from fear in the fact that it doesn't linger. "Spiking anxiety" comes on suddenly and generally leaves swiftly, depending on how soon one is away from the uncomfortable situation or how effectively it is handled. For example, when a person has misplaced his keys and he must get to work, his anxiety may soar. But when he finds them minutes later or phones work to let someone know he'll be late, his angst disappears. "Spiking anxiety" comes on so suddenly that most people act first and think later, but it should be the other way around.

Over the years, I've learned not to put a lot of stock into what people in society think about me. As long as you're not hurting anyone, I'd suggest you do the same. Start by learning your self-worth based on strengths, not weaknesses. Mentally go to the happiest time in your life and bring that forward. If you can't think of a happy time, imagine you are somewhere wonderful. Oftentimes you may think things seem impossible, but as exhibited in the movie *Mission: Impossible*, the impossible *is* possible.

People with dyslexia or other learning disabilities need to understand they are not failures just because they have a deficit. They should learn coping skills to deal with certain situations that will arise in life. Through years of trial and error, I've come up with methods to do so. These are some of my tips:

1. The best thing a student can do is inform his or her instructor of any limitations.

2. Ask the teacher to speak slowly and clearly to allow time for processing the information.

3. Request that words be printed on the board, as opposed to being written in cursive.

4. Have the teacher space letters, words, and numbers where they aren't jumbled or touching each other.

5. Ask the educator to leave what he or she has written

on the board so it can be photographed with a cell phone after class.

6. Since Roman numerals are especially difficult for one with dyslexia, ask that they be written clearly, along with the cardinal numbers next to them.

7. When studying for a test, highlight words with various colored highlighters to help you focus.

8. Use a Popsicle stick or invest in a bright, solid-colored bookmark to help you follow along in books as you read; both can help you focus on the words on one line and not others.

9. Purchase a magnifying glass or magnifying eyeglasses to make letters and words appear larger and easier to decipher.

10. Order magnifying sheets that can be placed over an entire page to assist with the clarity of written material.

11. Search and discover strengths and talents, and focus on those positives; they can greatly boost confidence in people with learning disabilities.

In America, we have some of the best, most caring teachers, and I believe they could be more dynamic if all were given tools to properly identify students with dyslexia and other learning disabilities. Through required workshops or continuing education classes, instructors could gain knowledge to arm themselves for what they may encounter and could be taught special techniques to effectively teach and encourage students with learning difficulties, thus eliminating a number of frustrations for all parties involved. Many times, children are mislabeled and get pushed aside or passed through to the next grade because educators simply lack the necessary skills to deal with them.

If parents detect their kid may have trouble learning, they should inform the teacher right away, and then fifty percent of the battle will have already been won. Yet some might not be aware of a child's problems until he or she enters school and may blame struggles on the instructor or school system. In turn, a teacher may place fault on parents. However, no one wins the blame game. Sometimes the problem is within the student and needs to be correctly identified so the appropriate help can be offered. Regardless of whether a parent or teacher is first to discover learning issues, he or she should inform the other. Doesn't every child deserve a fair chance???

Understanding the difference between right and left is a common problem for children with dyslexia. Parents can assist them. I recommend placing an apple and an orange on a table in front of the child. Have him or her grab the orange with the left hand. The adult should then move the position of both pieces of fruit and ask the youngster to grab the apple with the right hand. A piece of fruit can also be replaced with a favorite food, like a cookie. Continue practicing until the child grasps the concept.

To help with spelling, pronunciation, and memory, I

recommend my childhood game of writing one short word at a time on paper, cutting each letter out, then having the child or adult hide the letters in a room. Start with two-letter words, then progress to three, four, and five letters. Ask the child to count to twenty, and then the letter hunt begins! When all letters have been retrieved, have the child place them in order and sound out the word. It's like putting together a phonics puzzle. Parents or siblings can play the game too, which will make it more exciting. I've named this game "**Letter Hunt**."

Another fun method to help with pronunciation is to listen to song lyrics and try to memorize the words. Children can start with a nursery rhyme set to music and, as they get older, progress to their favorite songs. Writing down the lyrics can also improve spelling and can be checked using a dictionary. Plus, learning a song can create self-satisfaction.

A recorder can come in handy too, not only to document information you receive but ideas you don't want to forget. Of course, you can also record yourself pronouncing and spelling new or difficult words, and then play them back to help you master them.

Another problem for dyslexics of all ages is deciphering letters from numbers, especially when they have similar characteristics, such as **b** and **6**, **E** and **3**, **B** and **8**, and **I** and **1**. For children, I advise adults to write the alphabet on paper, alternating the letters with numbers, such as **A1B2C3D4**. First, have the child read all letters and numbers together as written. Second, ask him or her to repeat only the letters. Third, go back and have him or her say only the numbers. This form of training can help children learn the difference between the two. By doing so, they will be better prepared to read without their brains becoming so overwhelmed as they quickly try to fit each character into the number or letter category. This also cuts down on words and digits looking as if they are dancing on the page, out of control. Not only will the technique prepare kids for reading but it can boost confidence as well. Plus, it's a great lesson in following directions.

Similarly, grownups who are dyslexic often misinterpret numeric and alphabetic characters that bear resemblance, in turn causing words and numbers to seem to twist and spin like cast members of *Dancing with the Stars*. Adults, too, can immensely benefit from the practice of reading numbers and letters that have been written together, like those found in vehicle VIN numbers. For example, write **8B9O06** or **E3L7S5** and repeat each letter and number in order, aloud. Next, verbalize only the letters; then go back and voice only the numbers. With diligent practice, I've discovered this technique can help with the clarification of characters, making it less frustrating to read books, magazines, newspapers, paperwork, cards, and letters.

In addition, I suggest making a list of numbers and

letters on your cell phone or computer because they are often slightly different from those that are handwritten. Include characters such as **lL1Ii**. When you master those, write new patterns and practice saying them. We all know an NFL running back doesn't wait until the day of the game to train; much the same, a person with dyslexia or other learning disabilities needs to prepare ahead of time.

To give you a little insight into the world of dyslexia, I came up with this idea: Stare at your nose while holding a pencil out in front of you with the eraser approximately level with your lips. Continue staring at your nose, and you will likely see two pencils. If you focus a little longer, they will seem to move until they merge into one. I also call this method the **"Eye-Knows Game."** If you want to be creative, replace the pencil with a piece of paper and write a letter of the alphabet or a number on it. Using the same method as outlined above, you might notice the letter or number appears to be playing hopscotch. Now imagine spending your life seeing letters, numbers, and words this way.

By no means am I an expert in any area of education. My ideas come from a lifetime of experience living with learning disabilities.

Chapter Sixteen

The field of entertainment has intrigued me since I was a child. The older I became, the more I grew to love it, especially after performing in nursing homes; to this day, I still enjoy visiting and sometimes singing or dancing for the residents.

I have a lot of enthusiasm and drive to succeed in the world of the arts and entertainment, and I've been lucky enough to own a dance studio and model. I'm an okay dancer and model; I don't claim to be the best. When it comes to my dancing skills, I know there is always someone better, and I'm fine with that. In the past, I've competed in bodybuilding and was asked to appear on a local fitness television show now and again to share some of my nutrition and workout tips. Other times, I was called to judge pageants or dance competitions and was over the moon knowing someone had thought enough of me and my talent to value my judgment.

You may think I've reached my ultimate level of success. Although I am very happy with my achievements, I've never reached the level of success I desire. Yet have I stopped? No. Remember: I'm a nobody trying to be a somebody.

Because I was born with an extreme desire to succeed, I often felt doomed from the start. In a way, I wish my ambition hadn't been so strong, but if it hadn't, I wouldn't be writing this.

Ambition can be your friend or your enemy. For me, it was both. On one hand, it almost broke me, and on the other, it inspired me to achieve. I've always felt I was destined for bigger and better things. Some would say I was ripped off by having such a strong appetite for success while being plagued by the Ghost of Inability to Learn as well as dyslexia. As a child, no one knows the number of times I cried like a running faucet. I often wondered, *Why me? Why would God give me so much desire to succeed beyond my educational level?* All I know is, if I could receive an A for effort and ambition, I'm certain I would.

Hardships can either weaken or strengthen a person. If I weighed them all at once, I would feel powerless. Early on, I discovered piling up negatives combined with traumatic events only left a sense of being overwhelmed. Therefore, I learned to prioritize and try to handle life's punches one at a time; as a result, I have been able to move forward.

Looking back through adult eyes, I realize adversity has ultimately strengthened me, and in retrospect, my parents did an extraordinary job preparing me to handle it. If they hadn't, I wouldn't have been equipped for life's many challenges, such as my car being vandalized on one occasion and broken into at a mall and all of the Christmas gifts inside being stolen on another. Once my apartment was burglarized, and another time, it was burned due to someone else's negligence, resulting in the loss of irreplaceable items in both incidences. Additionally, a hurricane left a trail of community damage, affecting many I cared about and taking from them as well as myself. Moreover, after losing the greatest man in my life, my father, whom I highly respected, three very close people I looked up to also passed away, including my physician friend, who was not only a best friend but a father figure to me. Dealing with those and many other difficulties was not easy, but my upbringing provided me with the tools to cope. I had to accept what transpired, try not to dwell on the past, and move toward the future. My parents have shaped me into the man I am today, and for that I am grateful.

By writing this, I am not looking for sympathy. This book is destined to go places I've never been: around the world to the readers. I believe all people have something about themselves they don't like, whether they want to reveal it or not. Hopefully, they can find strength within this book and within themselves.

If God will extend my contract and allow me to remain here on earth a little while longer, I would like to inspire others to never give up, regardless of their afflictions or handicaps. They can overcome. Whether you are dyslexic, illiterate, blind, deaf, mute, autistic, in a wheelchair, or have ADHD or a disease, or have experienced a natural disaster or even a tragic break up, as long as you're still breathing, you can change your train of thought to a positive one. Even Mother Nature sends storms in our lives, but she also knows when to let the sun shine again. And we all need a little sunshine in our world.

For more insight into the author Likewise, visit:
www.Likewiseoriginal.com

Likewise Testimonials

"For the past 15 years, Alex Thomas has modeled in many annual bridal shows for us. Alex was born to be a performer, model, and dancer. He guides and assists other models with posing, turns, and does fabulous dance choreography. I highly recommend Alex to participate in any stage/runway production."

Brenda Carraway

"I am a supervisor at Rosewood Rehab and had the opportunity to work with Alex for six years. He was a very caring person and loved to entertain the residents. He would dress as the Easter Bunny and Santa Claus. Alex also took pride in his work while working here."

C. Witherspoon, ADON

"I have known Alex for over 8 years. During this time, I have been most impressed with many of his character attributes. His resilience, among other strengths, has been the most impressive. Despite the many pitfalls he has endured throughout life, his positive outlook has always shined through. I have been through certain events that have tried my spirit, but I have sought advice from Alex in the past. I have many "letters" after my name and you would think I could solve all of my problems (which pale in comparison to Alex's past trials), but look toward him for emotional strength and support."

Dr. Chris Lewis DVM, MS, CVSMT, CCRP, CVA

"My name is Dr. Andy Hillman and I am a veterinarian in Pensacola, Florida. I have had the pleasure of knowing Alex Thomas for over a decade. He is one of the most pleasant and delightful people I have ever met. When he visits my practice, he lifts the spirits of my staff with his positive energy and genuine personality. He is always courteous and never hesitates to jump in and lend a hand. I would endorse Alex for any position that requires charisma and charm, which he has in spades."

Dr. Andy Hillman

"My name is Robert Bellanova. I am the owner of Randall's Formal Wear here in Pensacola, Florida, and in Mobile, Alabama, for the past 35 years. I have been extremely fortunate to know Mr. Alex Thomas for over 20 of those years. He has modeled our formal wear and has danced during our bridal fashion shows during this time and has become one of clients', as well as our staff's, favorites!!! Alex has an infectious personality and is such a positive light to everyone he comes into contact with. He is an extraordinarily good listener and takes direction well, as well as an exemplary good leader. I can always count on Alex to take on any task assigned and he does it well—with much pride and dedication. In all my many years of knowing Alex, he has always maintained a sense of dignity, responsibility, and abundance when it comes to the consideration of others. Everyone Alex meets feels this way. He is a good and noble person who appears well in any company.

I know that Alex has had his own business for a while—teaching dance and fitness. Many of our mutual friends have commented on how patient and helpful Alex is while he directs his clients—this does not surprise me. Alex has always had a keen sense of duty and is a man of his word. Alex makes everyone in his company feel comfortable, worthy, and included.

If there is ever anything I can do as far as a

reference for Mr. Alex Thomas, please feel free to contact me. Alex has not only proved himself to me as someone dependable, honest, and courteous, but also someone I am extremely proud and honored to call 'friend.'"

Robert Bellanova

"The purpose of this letter is to provide a character reference for Alex Thomas who I have known as a friend and as close to a brother as one could ask. I first met Alex almost 20 years ago while living in Pensacola, FL. We were both volunteers at a charity event (one of many we worked together).

As a volunteer, Alex worked with young and old, always going above and beyond what was required and always with a smile on his face. He possesses a personality that exudes sensitivity, creativity, wisdom, and compassion. He is loyal, punctual, and well liked by all who come in contact. He has the ability to bring out the best in those around him and his mere presence has a calming effect in the most challenging situations.

Through our volunteer work, we became friends. My husband, a medical doctor, and I along with our children would often take family trips together with Alex. When my husband passed away Alex became a mentor to my children. He is the one who taught my sons (now 21 and 18) to be honorable, respectful, and resourceful young men. His infectious laughter, wonderful sense of humor combined with a strict moral code never waiver.

Alex has a strong ability to problem solve using common sense approaches. He never takes for granted the many skills and talents he has: dancing, singing, acting, cooking, etc. He is interested in the world around him and goes out of his way to continually improve himself.

As a friend and "brother," Alex Thomas has been incomparable. He is a loyal, honest, trustworthy, considerate individual who has the ability to see and understand things from another person's perspective. I could go on and on about Alex's strengths. In summary, in all he does, he brings integrity and would be an asset to anyone in any situation."

Liz Davis Rubin

Acknowledgments

A great team of people helped make this book possible. I would like to give acknowledgment to the following:

Dan Vega: Since I first walked into your office, you have been enthusiastic and supportive. Thank you for believing in me and giving me the opportunity to share my story with others. I am forever grateful!

Bobby Dunaway: You have not only been my liaison to the office but you have handled everything from answering my questions to posting my videos, all with the utmost patience, respect, and professionalism. A special thanks to you!

Earl Tillinghast: I respect your knowledge and skill as an editor. Your wisdom and guidance during the writing of this book have been invaluable. Thank you so much.

Hamishe Randall: You have been supportive from the beginning. Your suggestions, hard work, and editing have helped my story reach its full potential. I am very appreciative.

Velvet Skies (aka LuAnn Wibel): From the onset, you understood the importance of this story. I can never thank you enough for your time, dedication, patience, and writing skills. You have made this book what it is today. Thank you from the bottom of my heart!

My sincere gratitude goes to everyone behind the scenes at Indigo River Publishing.

Likewise

Contact Information for Specialized Assistance

International Dyslexia Association
40 York Road, 4th Floor
Baltimore, MD 21204
info@interdys.org
http://www.interdys.org
Tel: 410-296-0232; 800-ABC-D123

Learning Disabilities Association of America
4156 Library Road
Suite 1
Pittsburgh, PA 15234-1349
info@ldaamerica.org
http://www.ldaamerica.org
Tel: 412-341-1515

National Center for Learning Disabilities

32 Laight Street

Second Floor

New York, NY 10013

ncid@ncld.org

http://www.ncld.org

Tel: 212-545-7510; 888-575-7373

National Institute of Child Health and Human Development (NICHD)

National Institutes of Health, DHHS

31 Center Drive, Rm. 2A32 MSC 2425

Bethesda, MD 20892-2425

http://www.nichd.nih.gov

Tel: 301-496-5133

Fortunately, today there are many support groups for those with learning disabilities. You can speak with your doctor for suggestions to find one that will help you.

Velvet Skies (aka LuAnn Wibel) is from Foley, Alabama. She earned her bachelor's degree from the University of South Carolina and has spent the last eight years working as an educator in Pensacola, Florida.

Words from Velvet Skies about Likewise:

"I am extremely honored Likewise asked me to help write his book. He is strong, charismatic, optimistic, and very intelligent. I am confident people around the world, of various ages and backgrounds—regardless of social status or credentials—can learn from Likewise. He is truly wise beyond his years. I wish him all of the success he so greatly deserves!"